A TWITCHER'S DIARY

DIARY

THE BIRDWATCHING YEAR OF
RICHARD MILLINGTON

A TWITCHER'S DIARY

THE BIRDWATCHING YEAR OF
RICHARD MILLINGTON

BLANDFORD

BLANDFORD
An imprint of Cassell
Artillery House, Artillery Row,
London SW1P—1RT

First published 1981
This edition published 1990

Distributed in the United States by
Sterling Publishing Co. Inc.
387 Park Avenue South, New York,
NY—10016—8810

Distributed in Australia by
Capricorn Link (Australia) Pty Ltd
PO Box 665, Lane Cove, NSW 2066

British Library Cataloguing in Publication Data
Millington, Richard,
    A twitcher's diary.—2nd ed.
    1. Great Britain. Birds. Observation.
    I. Title
    598'.07'23441

ISBN 0—7137—2176—6

Colour reproduction by Culver Graphics Litho Ltd.
Typeset in Palatino
Printed in Yugoslavia by ČGP Delo
by arrangement with Papirografika

CONTENTS

A Twitcher's Great Britain

OUTER HEBRIDES

Tarbert

Lochmaddy
North Uist
Benbecula
South Uist

Vig

Skye

• Loch Garten
CAIRNGORMS

• Aberuthven

• Irvine

• Bamburgh

LAKE DISTRICT

Teesside •

New Brighton • Southport
Aber • Frodsham
Sheffield
Gringley on the Hill

Swallow Moss

Blithfield Res.

Cannock Chase

Draycote Res.

Higham Ferrers

SOUTH WALES

Stackpole
Oxwich
Blackpill
Peterstone
Worcester
Frampton
Slimbridge

Broxbourne •
Stocker's Lake •
Iver •
East Tilbury
Maldon
Great Wakering
Staines Res.
Elmley Marshes
Fleet Pond
Sandwich Bay
Dummer
Stadmarsh

Blagdon Lake
Chew Valley Res.
NEW FOREST
Dungeness

Dawlish Warren
Radipole
Davidstow Airport
Wadebridge
Totnes
Lodmoor
Portland Bill

Hayle Estuary
Marazion
Drift Res.
Porthgwarra
SCILLIES
Tresco St Martins
St Agnes St Mary's
Gugh
Veryan Bay
Gerrans Bay
Falmouth
Stithian's Res.
Slapton Ley
Prawle Point

The Wash inset

Cley Salthouse
Blakeney Point Quags
Holkham Weybourne Camp
Holme Titchwell Sheringham
THE WASH Salthouse Heath
Snettisham Lyng G P.s Waxham
King's Lynn Roydon Common THE BROADS Winterton
Norwich R. Yare
THE BRECKS Breydon Water
Welney E. Wretham
Mepal Thetford New Buckenham Lowestoft
Redisham Benacre
Livermere Walberswick
Minsmere
Sizewell
Wandlebury Mon. Levington Pools
Landguard Pt
Abberton Res.
Heybridge

[6]

PREFACE

In recent years there has been a tremendous increase in the number of people enjoying the hobby of birdwatching. It is an interest which can take many forms and many of the most enthusiastic birdwatchers soon become dedicated 'twitchers'.

A 'twitcher' is a birdwatcher who is fascinated by the variety of bird species that evolution has produced. He is prepared to travel extensively to try to see for himself as many different species as possible. He is a scientist, a sportsman and a conservationist, but above all he is a bird-fanatic. He 'collects' sightings of different birds by ticking them off on his list and cares deeply about the birds and their conservation—he wants to continue seeing as many different species as possible.

Twitchers keep lists of the birds they have seen, indeed in America they are known as 'listers'. For example, they keep life lists (of birds they have seen anywhere, ever), county lists (birds seen in a particular county) and British lists (birds seen in Britain). One of the most popularly kept lists is the British Year List—just a handful of the most dedicated twitchers have achieved the magic number of 300 species seen in Britain in a single year.

To see 200 bird species in a year in Britain is not too difficult, but to see 300 requires dedication—and the help of many other birdwatchers. The extra hundred species are made up of the rare visitors, some of which annually occur in Britain. Many of these birds appear just briefly at unpredictable and out-of-the-way places, so the twitcher must hear about them quickly, and then move fast before they have disappeared. Some of the rarest birds may appear in Britain just once and perhaps never again, so it is especially important to try not to miss seeing them. It may literally be the chance of a lifetime.

Most of these rare birds are relatively common species in other parts of the world, and they normally undergo long migrations. They are sometimes off course by thousands of miles when they appear in Britain. For example, it is not unknown for a bird which normally summers in Alaska and winters in South America to take a 'wrong turn' on the way and appear in Cornwall.

Twitchers cannot exist without the goodwill of the birdwatchers who are the lucky finders of the more exciting birds. It is these generous and unselfish birdwatchers who start the telephone 'grapevine' working, so that other people can come and enjoy the birds that they have found.

A certain amount of attack has been levelled at twitching on occasions, mainly from people who do not really understand it. It is sometimes something of a shock for a birdwatcher to find his usually quiet local spot invaded by crowds, but when the rare bird disappears so do the twitchers and the sighting has given a great deal of pleasure to many birdwatchers. Problems occasionally arise when an unusual number of birdwatchers descend on a site which has become temporary host to an extreme rarity, but very seldom is actual harm done, either to the birds or the habitat. Neither, generally, do twitchers disturb rare breeding birds. Most have a sound ornithological knowledge and therefore know how to watch even shy breeding birds without disturbing them.

A few more sedentary birdwatchers accuse twitchers of mindless competition and 'tick' collecting, and the fact that a certain amount of jargon is used tends to alienate some people. Some, self-explanatory occurs in this book, as it is part of the everyday vocabulary of a twitcher (for anyone requiring a more comprehensive glossary and an introduction to twitching in general Bill Oddie's *Little Black Bird Book* [Eyre Methuen, 1980] is recommended). But it must be stressed that—'tick' collecting and jargon apart—twitchers do fully appreciate the aesthetic quality of the birds. The keenest twitchers are undoubtedly bird-enthusiasts first and 'tick-hunters' second. They include amongst their ranks some of the best field ornithologists in the country. Lists are a way to catalogue some of the enjoyment of birdwatching and to provide personal achievement, as well as friendly competition. A bird is more than a 'tick'; it is a living wild creature that presents the birdwatcher with an absorbing and wonderful experience. If it is a species he has never seen before then the experience is all the more exciting.

Dedicated to—
The finders of rare birds—many whose names I do not know, but without whose unselfish attitude twitching could not exist and this book would not have been written. Thank you.

I would like to thank also—
Steve Gantlett, for his invaluable help in the preparation of this book, and without whose transport many of the birds may not have been seen; and
My wife, Hazel, who has the qualities of tolerance and understanding essential in a twitcher's partner.

[8]

SYSTEMATIC LIST OF BIRDS SEEN DURING YEAR

This list follows the nomenclature of Dr. K. H. Voous (1977, List of Recent Holarctic Bird Species)

GAVIIDAE Red-throated Diver *Gavia stellata*; Black-throated Diver *Gavia arctica*; Great Northern Diver *Gavia immer*.

PODICIPEDIDAE Pied-billed Grebe *Podilymbus podiceps*; Little Grebe *Tachybaptus ruficollis*; Great Crested Grebe *Podiceps cristatus*; Red-necked Grebe *Podiceps grisegena*; Slavonian Grebe *Podiceps auritus*; Black-necked Grebe *Podiceps nigricollis*.

PROCELLARIIDAE Fulmar *Fulmarus glacialis*; Cory's Shearwater *Calonectris diomedea*; Sooty Shearwater *Puffinus griseus*; Manx Shearwater *Puffinus puffinus*.

HYDROBATIDAE Storm Petrel *Hydrobates pelagicus*; Leach's Petrel *Oceanodroma leucorhoa*.

SULIDA Gannet *Sula bassana*.

PHALACROCORACIDAE Cormorant *Phalacrocorax carbo*; Shag *Phalacrocorax aristotelis*.

ARDEIDAE Bittern *Botaurus stellaris*; Little Egret *Egretta garzetta*; Grey Heron *Ardea cinerea*; Purple Heron *Ardea purpurea*.

CICONIIDAE Black Stork *Ciconia nigra*.

THRESKIORNITHIDAE Glossy Ibis *Plegadis falcinellus*; Spoonbill *Platalea leucorodia*.

ANATIDAE Mute Swan *Cygnus olor*; Bewick's Swan *Cygnus columbianus*; Whooper Swan *Cygnus cygnus*; Bean Goose *Anser fabalis*; Pink-footed Goose *Anser brachyrhynchus*; White-fronted Goose *Anser albifrons*; Greylag Goose *Anser anser*; Canada Goose *Branta canadensis*; Brent Goose *Branta bernicla*; Egyptian Goose *Alopochen aegyptiacus*; Shelduck *Tadorna tadorna*; Mandarin *Aix galericulata*; Wigeon *Anas penelope*; Gadwall *Anas strepera*; Teal *Anas crecca*; Mallard *Anas platyrhynchos*; Black Duck *Anas rubripes*; Pintail *Anas acuta*; Garganey *Anas querquedula*; Shoveler *Anas clypeata*; Red-crested Pochard *Netta ruffina*; Pochard *Aythya ferina*; Ring-necked Duck *Aythya collaris*; Ferruginous Duck *Aythya nyroca*; Tufted Duck *Aythya fuligula*; Scaup *Aythya marila*; Eider *Somateria mollissima*; Steller's Eider *Polysticta stelleri*; Long-tailed Duck *Clangula hyemalis*; Common Scoter *Melanitta nigra*; Velvet Scoter *Melanitta fusca*; Goldeneye *Bucephala clangula*; Smew *Mergus albellus*; Red-breasted Merganser *Mergus serrator*; Goosander *Mergus merganser*; Ruddy Duck *Oxyura jamaicensis*.

ACCIPITRIDAE Honey Buzzard *Pernis apivorus*; Red Kite *Milvus milvus*; Marsh Harrier *Circus aeruginosus*; Hen Harrier *Circus cyaneus*; Montagu's Harrier *Circus pygarus*; Goshawk *Accipiter gentilis*; Sparrowhawk *Accipiter nisus*; Buzzard *Buteo buteo*; Rough-legged Buzzard *Buteo lagopus*; Golden Eagle *Aquila chrysaetos*.

PANDIONIDAE Osprey *Pandion haliaetus*.

FALCONIDAE Kestrel *Falco tinnunculus*; Merlin *Falco columbarius*; Hobby *Falco subbuteo*; Peregrine *Falco peregrinus*.

TETRAONIDAE Red Grouse *Lagopus lagopus*; Black Grouse *Tetrao tetrix*; Capercaillie *Tetrao urogallus*.

PHASIANIDAE Red-legged Partridge *Alectoris rufa*; Grey Partridge *Perdix perdix*; Quail *Coturnix coturnix*; Pheasant *Phasianus colchicus*; Golden Pheasant *Chrysolophus pictus*; Lady Amherst's Pheasant *Chrysolophus amherstiae*.

RALLIDAE Water Rail *Rallus aquaticus*; Spotted Crake *Porzana porzana*; Corncrake *Crex crex*; Moorhen *Gallinula chloropus*; Coot *Fulica atra*.

[9]

GRUIDAE Crane *Grus grus.*

HAEMATOPODIDAE Oystercatcher *Haematopus ostralegus.*

RECURVIROSTRIDAE Black-winged Stilt *Himantopus himantopus*; Avocet *Recurvirostra avosetta.*

BURHINIDAE Stone-curlew *Burhinus oedicnemus.*

CHARADRIIDAE Little Ringed Plover *Charadrius dubius*; Ringed Plover *Charadrius hiaticula*; Kentish Plover *Charadrius alexandrinus*; Greater Sand Plover *Charadrius leschenaultii*; Dotterel *Charadrius morinellus*; Golden Plover *Pluvialis apricaria*; Grey Plover *Pluvialis squatarola*; Lapwing *Vanellus vanellus.*

SCOLOPACIDAE Knot *Calidris canutus*; Sanderling *Calidris alba*; Semipalmated Sandpiper *Calidris pusilla*; Little Stint *Calidris minuta*; Temminck's Stint *Calidris temminckii*; White-rumped Sandpiper *Calidris fuscicollis*; Baird's Sandpiper *Calidris bairdii*; Pectoral Sandpiper *Calidris melanotos*; Curlew Sandpiper *Calidris ferruginea*; Purple Sandpiper *Calidris maritima*; Dunlin *Calidris alpina*; Broad-billed Sandpiper *Limicola falcinellus*; Buff-breasted Sandpiper *Tryngites subruficollis*; Ruff *Philomachus pugnax*; Jack Snipe *Lymnocryptes minimus*; Snipe *Gallinago gallinago*; Woodcock *Scolopax rusticola*; Black-tailed Godwit *Limosa limosa*; Bar-tailed Godwit *Limosa lapponica*; Whimbrel *Numenius phaeopus*; Curlew *Numenius arquata*; Spotted Redshank *Tringa erythropus*; Redshank *Tringa totanus*; Greenshank *Tringa nebularia*; Lesser Yellowlegs *Tringa flavipes*; Solitary Sandpiper *Tringa solitaria*; Green Sandpiper *Tringa ochropus*; Wood Sandpiper *Tringa glareola*; Common Sandpiper *Actitis hypoleucos*; Spotted Sandpiper *Actitis macularia*; Turnstone *Arenaria interpres*; Wilson's Phalarope *Phalaropus tricolor*; Red-necked Phalarope *Phalaropus lobatus.*

STERCORARIIDAE Pomarine Skua *Stercorarius pomarinus*; Arctic Skua *Stercorarius parasiticus*; Long-tailed Skua *Stercorarius longicaudus*; Great Skua *Stercorarius skua.*

LARIDAE Mediterranean Gull *Larus melanocephalus*; Laughing Gull *Larus atricilla*; Franklin's Gull *Larus pipixcan*; Little Gull *Larus minutus*; Sabine's Gull *Larus sabini*; Black-headed Gull *Larus ridibundus*; Ring-billed Gull *Larus delawarensis*; Common Gull *Larus canus*; Lesser Black-backed Gull *Larus fuscus*; Herring Gull *Larus argentatus*; Iceland Gull *Larus glaucoides*; Glaucous Gull *Larus hyperboreus*; Great Black-backed Gull *Larus marinus*; Kittiwake *Rissa tridactyla*; Ivory Gull *Pagophila eburnea.*

STERNIDAE Gull-billed Tern *Gelochelidon nilotica*; Sandwich Tern *Sterna sandvicensis*; Roseate Tern *Sterna dougallii*; Common Tern *Sterna hirundo*; Arctic Tern *Sterna paradisaea*; Forster's Tern *Sterna forsteri*; Sooty Tern *Sterna fuscata*; Little Tern *Sterna albifrons*; Black Tern *Chlidonias niger.*

ALCIDAE Guillemot *Uria aalge*; Razorbill *Alca torda*; Black Guillemot *Cepphus grylle*; Little Auk *Alle alle*; Puffin *Fratercula arctica.*

COLUMBIDAE Rock Dove *Columba livia*; Stock Dove *Columba oenas*; Woodpigeon *Columba palumbus*; Collared Dove *Streptopelia decaocto*; Turtle Dove *Streptopelia turtur.*

CUCULIDAE Cuckoo *Cuculus canorus*; Yellow-billed Cuckoo *Coccyzus americanus.*

TYTONIDAE Barn Owl *Tyto alba.*

STRIGIDAE Scops Owl *Otus scops*; Little Owl *Athene noctua*; Tawny Owl *Strix aluco*; Long-eared Owl *Asio otus*; Short-eared Owl *Asio flammeus.*

CAPRIMULGIDAE Nightjar *Caprimulgus europaeus.*

APODIDAE Swift *Apus apus.*

ALCEDINIDAE Kingfisher *Alcedo atthis*; Belted Kingfisher *Ceryle alcyon.*

CORACIIDAE Roller *Coracias garrulus.*

UPUPIDAE Hoopoe *Upupa epops.*

PICIDAE Wryneck *Jynx torquilla*; Green Woodpecker *Picus viridis*; Great Spotted Woodpecker *Dendrocopus major*; Lesser Spotted Woodpecker *Dendrocopus minor.*

ALAUDIDAE Woodlark *Lullula arborea*; Skylark *Alauda arvensis*; Shore Lark *Eremophila alpestris.*

[10]

HIRUNDINIDAE Sand Martin *Riparia riparia*; Swallow *Hirundo rustica*; Red-rumped Swallow *Hirundo daurica*; House Martin *Delichon urbica*.

MOTACILLIDAE Richard's Pipit *Anthus novaeseelandiae*; Tawny Pipit *Anthus campestris*; Olive-backed Pipit *Anthus hodgsoni*; Tree Pipit *Anthus trivialis*; Meadow Pipit *Anthus pratensis*; Red-throated Pipit *Anthus cervinus*; Rock Pipit *Anthus spinoletta*; Yellow Wagtail *Motacilla flava*; Citrine Wagtail *Motacilla citreola*; Grey Wagtail *Motacilla cinerea*; Pied Wagtail *Motacilla alba*.

CINCLIDAE Dipper *Cinclus cinclus*.

TROGLODYTIDAE Wren *Troglodytes troglodytes*.

PRUNELLIDAE Dunnock *Prunella modularis*.

TURDIDAE Robin *Erithacus rubecula*; Nightingale *Luscinia megarhynchos*; Bluethroat *Luscinia svecica*; Black Redstart *Phoenicurus ochruros*; Redstart *Phoenicurus phoenicurus*; Whinchat *Saxicola rubetra*; Stonechat *Saxicola torquata*; Wheatear *Oenanthe oenanthe*; Ring Ouzel *Turdus torquatus*; Blackbird *Turdus merula*; Fieldfare *Turdus pilaris*; Song Thrush *Turdus philomelos*; Redwing *Turdus iliacus*; Mistle Thrush *Turdus viscivorus*.

SYLVIIDAE Cetti's Warbler *Cettia cetti*; Grasshopper Warbler *Locustella naevia*; Savi's Warbler *Locustella luscinioides*; Aquatic Warbler *Acrocephalus paludicola*; Sedge Warbler *Acrocephalus schoenobaenus*; Marsh Warbler *Acrocephalus palustris*; Reed Warbler *Acrocephalus scirpaceus*; Great Reed Warbler *Acrocephalus arundinaceus*; Booted Warbler *Hippolais caligata*; Icterine Warbler *Hippolais icterina*; Melodious Warbler *Hippolais polyglotta*; Dartford Warbler *Sylvia undata*; Subalpine Warbler *Sylvia cantillans*; Sardinian Warbler *Sylvia melanocephala*; Barred Warbler *Sylvia nisoria*; Lesser Whitethroat *Sylvia curruca*; Whitethroat *Sylvia communis*; Garden Warbler *Sylvia borin*; Blackcap *Sylvia atricapilla*; Pallas's Warbler *Phylloscopus proregulus*; Yellow-browed Warbler *Phylloscopus inornatus*; Wood Warbler *Phylloscopus sibilatrix*; Chiffchaff *Phylloscopus collybita*; Willow Warbler *Phylloscopus trochilus*; Goldcrest *Regulus regulus*; Firecrest *Regulus ignicapillus*.

MUSCICAPIDAE Spotted Flycatcher *Muscicapa striata*; Red-breasted Flycatcher *Ficedula parva*; Pied Flycatcher *Ficedula hypoleuca*.

TIMALIIDAE Bearded Tit *Panurus biarmicus*.

AEGITHALIDAE Long-tailed Tit *Aegithalos caudatus*.

PARIDAE Marsh Tit *Parus palustris*; Willow Tit *Parus montanus*; Crested Tit *Parus cristatus*; Coal Tit *Parus ater*; Blue Tit *Parus caeruleus*; Great Tit *Parus major*.

SITTIDAE Nuthatch *Sitta europaea*.

CERTHIIDAE Treecreeper *Certhia familiaris*.

ORIOLIDAE Golden Oriole *Oriolus oriolus*.

LANIIDAE Isabelline Shrike *Lanius isabellinus*; Red-backed Shrike *Lanius collurio*; Great Grey Shrike *Lanius excubitor*; Woodchat Shrike *Lanius senator*.

CORVIDAE Jay *Garrulus glandarius*; Magpie *Pica pica*; Chough *Pyrrhocorax pyrrhocorax*; Jackdaw *Corvus monedula*; Rook *Corvus frugilegus*; Carrion Crow *Corvus corone*; Raven *Corvus corax*.

STURNIDAE Starling *Sturnus vulgaris*; Rose-coloured Starling *Sturnus roseus*.

PASSERIDAE House Sparrow *Passer domesticus*; Tree Sparrow *Passer montanus*.

VIREONIDAE Red-eyed Vireo *Vireo olivaceus*.

FRINGILLIDAE Chaffinch *Fringilla coelebs*; Brambling *Fringilla montifringilla*; Greenfinch *Carduelis chloris*; Goldfinch *Carduelis carduelis*; Siskin *Carduelis spinus*; Linnet *Carduelis cannabina*; Twite *Carduelis flavirostris*; Redpoll *Carduelis flammea*; Two-barred Crossbill *Loxia leucoptera*; Crossbill *Loxia curvirostra*; Scarlet Rosefinch *Carpodacus erythrinus*; Bullfinch *Pyrrhula pyrrhula*; Hawfinch *Coccothraustes coccothraustes*.

EMBERIZIDAE Lapland Bunting *Calcarius lapponicus*; Snow Bunting *Plectrophenax nivalis*; Yellowhammer *Emberiza citrinella*; Cirl Bunting *Emberiza cirlus*; Ortolan Bunting *Emberiza hortulana*; Reed Bunting *Emberiza schoeniclus*; Corn Bunting *Miliaria calandra*.

THE DIARY

dull and cloudy

Hazelslade, Cannock Chase, Staffs

The ♂ Two-barred Crossbill located with small party of Crossbills, in oak trees around drinking pool in clearing. Watched feeding later on larch cones, at edge of plantation. Seen to be perhaps neater in proportions than the accompanying Crossbills, with rounder head-shape. Plumage clean, quite pale salmony-pink, lacking the 'burnt' quality of ♂ Crossbill, with slightly darker mantle and minimal streaking on flanks. Some blue-grey under-feathering occasionally showing on 'shoulders'. Black wings with striking, broad, white double wing-bars and white tips to tertials, the former obvious at great distances and in flight. Shortish, notched, black tail. Eyes dark, bill and legs dark brown.

Also several Siskins and Redpolls seen, and a total of 30+ Crossbills in parties around the clearing.

Two-barred Crossbill. Normally sedentary in the sub-Arctic forests, but irregularly irruptive—then occurring rarely in western Europe, with perhaps less than 60 birds recorded in Britain.

East Bank, Cley, Norfolk

Ten Goldeneye and a single Spotted Redshank on Arnold's Marsh, the latter in silvery winter plumage. Also 1 Red-throated Diver flying past at sea, and 1 Kingfisher fishing along the drainage ditch, but few other birds of note, with no sign of the reported Black Guillemot.

Travelling near Plymouth 1 Tawny Owl seen perched on crash-barrier beside main road.

Wadebridge, Cornwall   08.00

The Belted Kingfisher, having proved most elusive last November, now performing in the most exemplary fashion—seen immediately, perched on telegraph wires over the river and watched down to 40 yards in bright sunshine, catching and eating several small flatfish. Huge, Jackdaw-sized, kingfisher with plumage air-force blue above, white below with broad blackish breast-band. Large-headed with upstanding shaggy crest and strong bill. White spot in front of eye and narrow white tips to secondaries and primaries noticeable at close range, similarly rufous smudging on sides of breast. Rather reminiscent of Hoopoe in flight, with peculiar uneven wing-beats, and showing white flash at base of primaries. Called several times—a loud 'wooden' rattle.

Belted Kingfisher. North America. Only the second ever to be recorded in Britain, the other apparently at the same place in 1908.

[13]

Totnes, Devon   12.00

Two immature Ring-necked Ducks diving with 15+ Tufted Ducks on river at Dartington Weir. Quite distinctive shape of head with high, knobbed, rear crown. Plumage generally dark ashy-brown with paler flanks, curling up in front of closed wing. Off-white patch at base of bill and white eye-ring, extending as a line back from eye. Blue-grey bill with white band near tip. Broad pale grey wing-bar also noted, while preening.

Ring-necked Duck. North America. Formerly very rare, first recorded in 1957 but in last few years occurring annually, with some 90 records, 25 being in the last year alone.

Portland Harbour, Dorset   14.15

Several Red-breasted Mergansers. One Slavonian Grebe and 1 Red-necked Grebe diving, out in harbour.

One ♀ Stonechat perched on weeds in Ferrybridge car park.

Two Little Auks watched swimming and diving just offshore, in harbour—tiny, dumpy auks in immaculate black and white winter plumage. Characteristic thick-set neck, rounded head and stubby bill giving a 'double-ended' appearance. White 'eyelids' and mantle streaks noticeable at short range.

Little Auk. Breeding in Arctic Atlantic, pelagic in winter; occasionally found in coastal waters, usually after severe gales.

[14]

Ferrybridge, Dorset
One winter-plumaged Red-necked Grebe swimming very close to main road, in the Fleet. Medium-sized grebe with dusky face, neck and flanks and distinctive yellow-based bill.

Red-necked Grebe. Regular winter visitor, in small numbers, mostly in the South and East.

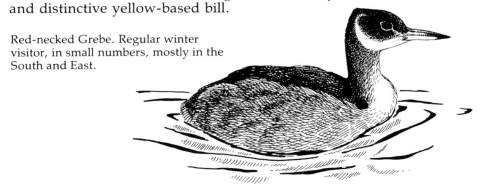

Radipole Lake, Dorset
One first-winter Glaucous Gull on edge of mud island in lake, preening and resting with about 450 Black-headed Gulls. Very large, 'milky-coffee'-coloured gull with shortish, white primaries. Square-headed with mean expression and heavy pink bill showing sharply demarcated dark brown tip.

Glaucous Gull. Regular winter visitor in small numbers from the Arctic (mostly to northern coastal ports).

One Little Owl of fierce disposition picked from roadside near Bere Regis after collision with a car at dusk.

[15]

Chiswell Cove, Portland, Dorset 08.15

Close views of the immature Ivory Gull were obtained, the bird resting for much of the time on the beach at Randy Row. Also watched feeding on fish scraps, as well as flying up and down the shoreline. Rather awkward looking bird on the ground, with pigeon-chested, round-headed and short-legged appearance but contrastingly graceful in flight, with long wings and fan-tail. Plumage pure white with slight grey flecks on nape, small blackish spots on mantle and wing coverts, and neat blackish tips to wing feathers. Also dark subterminal spotting on tail feathers noted in flight. Dirty-grey smudging on face extending from base of bill onto forehead, cheeks and chin, but with white 'eyelids'. Dark eye, black legs and feet, and smallish grey-green bill with peach-coloured tip.

After performing for about an hour, the bird flew off onto the rocks at the base of Portland's west cliffs.

Ivory Gull. Confined to the high Arctic, rarely straying in winter from the edge of the pack-ice. Occurs as a winter vagrant to Britain, usually in the northern isles. Very rare in recent years.

Radipole Lake, Weymouth, Dorset 09.15

Extensive searching of the area for the next seven hours eventually produced the required result—superb views of the winter-plumaged Pied-billed Grebe. 'Scoped in the last of the bright sunshine, the bird was fishing with several Little Grebes in a small weed-fringed ditch adjoining the river. Seen to be distinctly larger and more angular than Little Grebe, with a spiky tail, and darker and greyer in colour. Plumage generally dusky brown on mantle, nape and crown, paler on cheeks, neck and flanks. Sides of upper neck noted as being a warmer, rusty-brown colour; indeed the general appearance of the bird was vaguely reminiscent of Red-necked Grebe. Also showing a narrow whitish eye-ring, white throat and white under-tail coverts. The bill, relatively stout and blunt, appeared to be pale fleshy-grey in colour, with a dark band near tip, wider on lower mandible.

An excellent encounter with a most shy and retiring bird—quite a contrast with the other of today's mega-cripplers.

Pied-billed Grebe. North and South America, migrant and wanderer, with only a handful of British records, all since 1963.

Few other birds of note were seen during the day, apart from several Water Rails, Bearded Tits, Reed Buntings and 1 Cetti's Warbler, watched feeding along the river's edge.

[17]

Kilverstone Heath, The Brecks, Norfolk   15.30

Three ♂ and 5 ♀.Golden Pheasants watched feeding nervously along edge of ploughed field beside pinewood. The males resplendent in their gaudy red, yellow, black and orange plumage; the females rather dull, but noticeably smaller and more richly coloured than ♀ Pheasant.

Golden Pheasant. Now a well-established introduced species, mostly in East Anglia and southern Scotland.

Slimbridge, Glos   09.30–12.30

About 1,000 White-fronted Geese grazing on and around the tackpiece, gradually moving off towards distant fields. Also 3 Brent Geese, with the White-fronts, about 100 Bewick's Swans, mostly on Rushy Pen, and many Wigeon, but few other wild birds of note.

Ruddy Duck. Originally from North America, introduced birds have colonised much of west and central England and now appear to be naturalised as British birds.

Chew Valley Lake, Avon   13.30–16.00

Many duck around reservoir, including Wigeon, Teal, Shovelers, Tufted Ducks and Pochard. Also 5+ Goosanders and at least 8 Ruddy Ducks, two of the latter being quite good chestnut-plumaged males. Many Lapwings and Snipe around the shoreline, and 15 Dunlins.

Greater Sand Plover. West and central Asia, wintering widely from South Africa to Australia. This is the second bird recorded in Britain, the first being in Sussex the previous winter.

The winter-plumaged/juvenile Greater Sand Plover located feeding, with typical 'tipping' plover action, in large damp grassy field with 150 Lapwings. Quite large, top-heavy 'ringed' plover with sharply tapered rear end and longish, quite heavy, black bill. Hunched, 'chick-like' stance with longish grey-green legs. Generally pale plumage, greyish-brown above with pale wing coverts noticeable at some range, darker brown cheek and breast patches, and whitish supercilium and fore-head. No white collar, all white below.

Blagdon Lake, Avon   16.10

Very little apart from 1 ♀ Goldeneye and 1 fine ♂ Smew close to dam.

———————————————February 5———————————————

Very little at Slimbridge but for a few White-fronts and Bewick's Swans, and nothing of note at Stanpit, Dorset. The lack of Lesser White-front and Serin both, constitutes a double dip day.

Harleston Gravel Pits, Suffolk   13.30

One ♂ and 3 red-head Goosanders swimming on main lake, the male in fine plumage with creamy flanks and green-glossed head.

Walberswick Marshes, Suffolk   14.00

Two Lesser Spotted Woodpeckers at top of oak trees near Lodge, indulging in weird posturing and uttering odd, slurred calls.

Two or three ringtail Hen Harriers hunting over marshes and farm-land nearby, and 1 ♂ Merlin perched on top of small bush at edge of reed-beds.

Party of 9 Bewick's Swans flew over, south.

About 15 Common Scoters and 5 Great Crested Grebes on sea, and 1 Knot along shoreline.

Lesser Spotted Woodpecker. Resident, though with local distribution, in England and Wales only.

Rough-legged Buzzard. Breeding in the sub-Arctic and Arctic tundra, a scarce winter visitor to Britain, usually in the North and East.

A Rough-legged Buzzard landed close to road, in grassy field near the water tower. Watched at very close range on the ground before it flew off to hedgerow trees. From here the bird continued hunting, perched precariously on top of small trees and occasionally dropping down into field. Flew off south across marsh at dusk.

One Little Owl perched on roadside tree near Halesworth 17.30.

Cley, Norfolk   08.30

Shore Larks (15+) feeding along shingle beach near North Hide—
quite pale buffy-grey birds with fairly clear-cut yellow and black face-
pattern.

Also 25+ Chaffinches and 5 Snow Buntings feeding on shingle here.
A party of about 20 Snow Buntings flew east overhead with characteristic delicate ringing and trilling calls.

Party of 8 Lapland Buntings watched feeding in the Eye field, creeping amongst the grass tussocks in mouse-like fashion. Pale-headed
appearance, with dark 'cheek-corners'; rufous nape and wing panels,
long wings and short tail noted.

Shore Lark. This species breeds from
Scandinavia eastwards, in the Arctic
tundra, regularly wintering in small
numbers on Britain's east coast.

Lapland Bunting. Usually an autumn
passage migrant in Britain with only a
few wintering, on the east coast.

Holkham, Norfolk

One Jack Snipe flushed from ditch by caravan site, showing relatively
short bill, domed head and dark tail.

Party of about 120 White-fronted Geese grazing out on the freshmarsh.

Titchwell, Norfolk

Five or more Velvet Scoters with 40+ Common Scoters in scattered raft
offshore. Mostly females, the former showing double pale face patches,
long-headed appearance and white wing patches. Also 5 Goldeneye on
sea and 75 Knot along shoreline, including 2 'punk'-dyed birds with
bright green under-parts.

Several Red-breasted Mergansers and Eiders off Hunstanton, but
otherwise few birds of note during rest of the day, at Roydon Common
or East Wretham.

[23]

East Wretham Heath, Norfolk

Several Marsh, Willow, Coal, Blue and Long-tailed Tits in bushes. One Tawny Owl hooting from beechwood on heath, and 1 Treecreeper.

Fifteen Hawfinches seen around ponds and along back of heath after fog cleared in mid-morning. Very vocal, constantly uttering sharp 'tzik' and 'tsee' calls, and very timid, though several birds seen well, feeding on ground under stand of hornbeams. Heavy-looking birds with very stout bills, brown mantle, pinkish under-parts, orangy head and contrasting pale grey nape and white wing patches. In flight showing conspicuous white patterning on tail and (otherwise dark) wings. Most birds with off-white bills, but one male showing steely-grey bill.

Hawfinch. Fairly scarce resident in most of Britain, south of central Scotland, its shy habits rendering it difficult to locate away from the traditional winter gathering sites.

Also 2 Golden Plovers over, calling, and 1 ♂ Sparrowhawk along hedge, flushing many Blackbirds, Woodpigeons, Jays and even Pheasants from field edge.

Harleston Gravel Pits, Suffolk   13.00

Several Great Crested Grebes and 1 ♂ Goosander the only birds of interest, apart from one, presumably feral, Bean Goose with a party of Canada Geese.

Walberswick Marshes, Suffolk

One or two Hen Harriers quartering reed-beds and heath, occasionally soaring, and 1 ♀ Merlin on bushes in reeds, and flying around briefly.

One Goshawk soaring over valley, moving down towards the sea before powering off northwards. Although vaguely similar to huge Sparrowhawk in coloration, quite different in shape with rather projecting head, longish, fairly pointed wings in straight flight, these held flat (or even slightly decurved) while circling. White under-tail coverts not particularly noticeable.

Goshawk. Widespread in Europe, but apart from perhaps a few resident birds in Britain, occurs only as a rare autumn and winter visitor.

Minsmere, Suffolk   15.30
The usual selection of ducks and waders, also Black-tailed Godwit and 1 Spotted Redshank, on the scrape. Also 1 Marsh Harrier over reeds and a superb Barn Owl, hunting over the near edge of the scrape, at dusk.

February 24 — dull and misty

Slimbridge, Glos   09.00
A few Brent Geese and 2+ Pink-footed Geese located amongst about 2,000 White-fronted Geese, but missed the Lesser White-front again, due to mis-timed tea injection.

Pink-footed Goose. Winter visitor in large numbers mostly to northern England and southern Scotland.

[25]

Roydon Common, Norfolk   14.30
Great Grey Shrike located on top of small birch saplings out on common. It soon moved much closer, and was heard to be singing. Fine, clean, grey, black and white bird, washed with pink on under-side.

Great Grey Shrike. Scarce winter visitor and passage migrant, mostly in eastern coastal areas and selected traditional inland sites.

Snettisham, Norfolk   15.30
About 20 Goldeneye on gravel pits, including several displaying males. A few other ducks including Gadwall and 1 Red-breasted Merganser. Also lots of Grey Partridges. Thousands of waders, pushed up onto mud by rising tide in the Wash, the majority being Dunlin and Knot.

Roydon Common, Norfolk   16.30
Two ♂ Merlins—1 very orangy below, this remaining perched for the whole evening on a close signpost, while the second bird dashed around in the distance. Two adult male Hen Harriers came in, separately, to roost, both sporting neat, pale grey, white and black coloration, with prominent white rump and dark trailing edges to secondaries.

Hen Harrier. Breeds in north-west Britain. A winter visitor and passage migrant elsewhere.

[26]

Aber, Gwynedd   07.30

One very confiding Dipper watched on river flowing across beach, perched on rock, bobbing. Plump, sleek-plumaged bird showing scaly pattern on upper-parts. Flew upriver, calling—loud metallic 'zink'.

Dipper. Resident on rocky, fast-flowing rivers in north and west Britain.

Black Duck. North America. Less than a dozen have been recorded in Britain and Ireland. Capable of interbreeding freely with Mallard, there are hybrids appearing in Britain as a result of this bird and the Scillies female, apparently making themselves fully at home.

The ♂ Black Duck located in channel at river mouth walked out onto mudflats with a ♀ Mallard, providing excellent comparison. Seen to be larger than Mallard, with perhaps longer neck and legs. Plumage generally very dark, mottled blackish-brown body, paler buffish on face and neck with dark crown, eye-stripe and nape. Dull yellowish bill; legs and feet reddish-orange. Flew out to tide edge, to join other ducks, showing dark speculum and flashing white under-wings.

Also 1 Buzzard soaring over hillside, mobbed by Raven.

Llanfairfechan Sewage Farm, Gwynedd   09.30

One or 2 Firecrests flitting around in trees beside track—as usual, bright little birds with white supercilia and bronzey shoulder patches. Nuthatch, too.

North Wales

One Peregrine, located by chance, perched on rocky outcrop, with puffed out, very pinkish, under-parts. A second bird flew in, circling around hillside—a ♂ with very blue-cast upper-parts—dangling its large, bright yellow, feet. Both birds watched perched separately on hillside, and soaring overhead, with a Raven.

New Brighton, Merseyside 13.00

Several waders on exposed mud, including Sanderling, and 4 Purple Sandpipers feeding on seaweed-covered rocks.

Many gulls started appearing along the beach as tide ebbed, mostly Black-headed, Herring and Common Gulls, several Lesser and a few Great Black-backs. One adult Mediterranean Gull found standing amongst resting Black-headed Gulls—very pale mantle, white primaries and heavy blackish head markings, also bright red drooping bill noted. The adult Iceland Gull appeared on sandy shore near sewage outfall when this was cleared by the tide—long white primaries, 'soft' expression and medium yellow bill with red spot.

Iceland Gull. Fairly scarce winter visitor, this particular individual traditionally returning every winter to New Brighton.

Mediterranean Gull. An increasingly regular visitor, mostly in winter, and usually to southern Britain.

[28]

Norfolk Broads   07.30–15.00

After exhaustive searching, the 3 Cranes were eventually seen, at some distance, feeding in an area of damp fields. Apparently adults, unmistakable creatures at any range, being very tall and grey with black and white patterned head. Drooping plumes obscuring tail.

Few other birds of note except 1 Marsh Harrier over one of the meres, and several Bearded Tits.

Crane. Summer visitor to north and central Eurasia, normally occurring in Britain only as a very rare, though annual, passage migrant.

Stocker's Lake, Rickmansworth, Herts   15.00

One semi-albino Dunnock on path and in bushes, showing most disconcerting snowy-white crown, face and nape.

About 50 Shovelers and 20+ Goldeneyes on gravel pits, with over 100 Tufted Ducks and 30 Pochards. Three Red-crested Pochards swimming around in corner, including 2 adult ♂ in gaudy plumage, with orangy head, black, white and brown body and crimson bill.

Little Britain Lake, Iver, Bucks

One ♂ Ferruginous Duck on small lake, spending much time under overhanging branches beside islands. Quite small duck, neatly proportioned with rather peaked crown. Plumage rich mahogany brown with darker mantle, relieved by clear-cut white under-tail coverts and white eye, blue bill.

Red-crested Pochard. Range spreading in Europe, now annually seen in Britain in autumn and winter, but popular as an ornamental waterfowl — many are doubtless escapes from captivity.

Ferruginous Duck. Another duck often kept in captivity, but a few do appear to be genuine winter visitors, from southern Europe and central Asia.

Staines Reservoir, Middx   17.00

Four (1 ♂) Goosanders and 10 (4 ♂) Goldeneye on southern part of reservoir, with many Tufted Duck, Pochard and Wigeon.

Two Smew on northern side, 1 immaculate black and white ♂ and 1 'redhead'—grey bodied with dark chestnut head showing pure white face and throat.

Smew. Scarce winter visitor from northern Russia, traditionally found on the London reservoirs.

March 15

Four separate Barn Owls beside the road, in car headlights, between Plymouth and Bodmin, around 02.00.

Falmouth, Cornwall   07.00

The winter-plumaged Forster's Tern watched fishing, commuting between bays, before being grilled on rocks just offshore in Swanpool Bay. Flew with quite shallow wing-beats, perhaps reminiscent of the marsh terns, also diving sharply for fish and capable of quick turns of flight to out-manoeuvre marauding Herring Gulls. In flight, mantle and tail very pale grey, wings pale grey, lighter on inner primaries and secondaries, darker on forewing and outer primaries, latter with dark tips. Appeared white-headed with black mask and long bill. Perched, head pattern distinctive—white with bold black mask through eye, wider on cheeks, fine black speckling across nape appearing as a light grey wash at distance. Grey and white patterned primary tips and dark-centred tertails/inner secondaries also noted at rest. Relatively long bill, black, slightly reddish at base of lower mandible, and quite long legs yellowy-orange in colour.

Also Fulmars and a Gannet flying, out in bay, 3+ winter-plumaged Razorbills and 1 winter-plumaged Little Auk diving in bay. One Mute Swan on sea.

Forster's Tern. Southern United States. The first ever record in Britain, certainly qualifying as a mega-tick.

[31]

An immature Mediterranean Gull was also standing on the rocks in the bay, and flying—pale grey mantle contrasting with all-dark outer primaries and bar on secondaries. Stout bill dark brown with horn-coloured base.

First-winter Mediterranean Gull. The incidence of juveniles appears to be greater in recent years, due partly to the spread of the species and partly to increasing competence at field identification amongst birdwatchers.

South Devon

Six Slavonian Grebes—1 in Gerran's Bay, 1 on Slapton Ley and 4 at Dawlish; all in winter plumage, but two at Dawlish moulting into summer plumage, showing dark necks, grey-smudged cheeks, dusky flanks and peaked rear crowns—very similar overall to Black-necked Grebe, but for bill shape.

Also a flock of 15+ Black-throated Divers in Veryan Bay—very dark black-and-white-looking, but with pale rear flanks, straight bill and dark grey crown and nape.

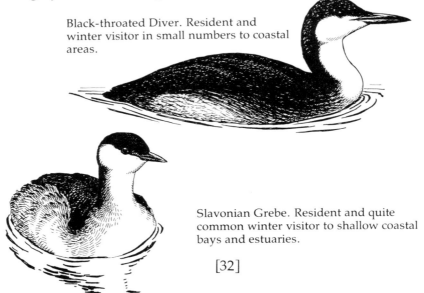

Black-throated Diver. Resident and winter visitor in small numbers to coastal areas.

Slavonian Grebe. Resident and quite common winter visitor to shallow coastal bays and estuaries.

[32]

One female Cirl Bunting, feeding on grassy embankment and perched in trees, calling—a thin but penetrating 'sseet'. Compact bird, a much-streaked version of ♂ with broken head-pattern and dull olivy rump.

Cirl Bunting. In Britain it is locally distributed, mainly in the south and south-west coastal counties.

March 16

South Wales
Over 100 summer-plumaged Guillemots and Razorbills around cliffs, with other seabirds, including Shags, Kittiwakes and Fulmars. Pair of Peregrines 'scoped perched on clifftop crags—broad-shouldered falcons with bluish upper-parts, creamy below with transverse barring. Distinctive head pattern—white cheeks and broad black moustachials.

Peregrine Falcon. Local resident on sea-cliffs and mountains in northern and western Britain.

[33]

Several parties of Jackdaws around cliffs, and a pair of Ravens flew from headland, croaking.

Two Choughs 'switchbacking' along, off cliff-face, drifting up and over headland, calling—a high-pitched, penetrating 'chee-arr'. Very glossy plumage, square-cut wings and tail, bright red decurved bill and red legs noted.

Several Stonechats on clifftop gorse-bushes, singing.

Chough. Scarce resident, its British stronghold being in west Wales, with a few in Scotland and Isle of Man.

Mid Wales   11.00

Five variously coloured Buzzards and 1 Raven over road.

One Kingfisher flew upriver beside road.

One Red Kite floating around over hilltop with 4 Buzzards—seen to be larger and far more elegant in flight with long, angled wings and long, freely animated, forked tail. Orangy-russet body and tail, pale head and dark wings noted, latter with contrasting white area on under-side of primaries and creamy bar on upper-side. A very hand-some bird.

Red Kite. Though widespread in Europe, a very rare migrant in Britain away from the small resident population in Wales.

Blackpill, West Glam   14.30

Nothing but lots of gulls.

[34]

Norfolk Broads
One Short-eared Owl hunting over pasture land beside river, on long, curiously stiffly held, wings. Pale buffy-brown, blotched dark brown with orange primary flashes, and dark carpal patches noted. Tail broadly barred dark brown.

The 3 adult Cranes located immediately, feeding in a partly cleared potato field about 200 yards from main road, providing much more satisfactory views than on March 4, and extra features noted, including horn-coloured bill and small black bar at rear of closed wing.

Two Red-throated Divers on sea at Sea-Palling.

Cley, Norfolk   11.00
A walk around the reserve produced 10+ Ruffs, 1 Spotted Redshank and 2 newly-arrived Avocets, as well as 200 Brent Geese grazing in damp fields and the usual Gadwalls, Shovelers and Teal, etc.

One Twite feeding on weeds beside East Bank—a dark Linnet-like finch with buffy face and yellow bill, and dull pink rump.

One Lapland Bunting flew over and landed in Eye field, calling—a flat, toneless rattle—'ticitrrk'.

One Short-eared Owl flew in, high over reserve, landing on grassy island in New scrape.

Little else seen, except a ♂ Kestrel despatching a common lizard on East Bank.

Twite. Though breeding in northern Britain, present only in winter on the coastal saltmarshes of eastern England; some are probably continental birds.

_____*April 5*_____

New Buckenham, Norfolk
The first Swallow, hawking over cornfields behind the house, heralding the spring.

Swallow. Common summer visitor, wintering in South Africa.

[35]

Cley, Norfolk 12.00

Now far more waders on reserve, including about 50 Dunlin, about 15 Ruff, 3 Grey Plovers, 1 summer-plumaged Black-tailed Godwit and 1 Spotted Redshank. Also 20+ Avocets, displaying, and many Teal, Shelducks, Gadwall, about 40 Wigeon, 10 Shovelers and 1 pair of Pintail. 1 Bittern booming from reed-beds all afternoon, and several Bearded Tits calling.

Salthouse Heath, Norfolk

One Long-eared Owl calling at dusk—a very soft, low, repeated hoot. Seen flying casually amongst the trunks, calling.

One Tawny Owl hooting, and 2 Woodcocks flushed from edge of path.

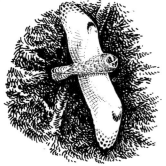

Long-eared Owl. Locally distributed resident over much of Britain, and a passage migrant.

Cley, Norfolk 08.00

One Bittern booming and the same ducks and waders as yesterday; also 40 partial summer-plumaged Golden Plovers in the Eye field.

1 Sparrowhawk flew west, high over reserve.

Several newly-arrived summer visitors, including an early Sedge Warbler singing from brambles beside road, 1 Chiffchaff singing, and 1 Wheatear by North Hide. Other migrants included a party of 7 Siskins and 1 Grey Wagtail flying west.

Holkham Pines (West end), Norfolk 11.00

One very grey ♂ Merlin flew from bushes beside track and quickly off across freshmarsh. Later one Firecrest flitting along edge of path, in bushes, calling—repeated, sharp 'zeet'. A particularly bright individual, with characteristic golden 'cape' and strongly striped head.

Firecrest. Though breeding in very small numbers in widely scattered localities, it is a scarce but regular passage migrant along the east and south coasts.

[36]

One Crossbill flew over, calling—repeated, hard, insistent 'chip, chip'.

Few migrants but for 5 singing Chiffchaffs, 6 Fieldfares flying over north, and 1 Wheatear on dunes.

Thirty-five feral Greylag Geese and 1 Egyptian Goose grazing in fields beside road.

Winterton Dunes, Norfolk   15.00

No sign of the reported Richard's Pipit, and few other birds besides 4 Stonechats, 1 Wheatear and 2 Bramblings—the latter feeding in sheep paddocks with 25+ Yellowhammers.

SE4	*April 12*	clear and sunny

Cley, Norfolk   14.30

A few winter visitors still in evidence—3 Redwings flew east, and 1 ringtail Hen Harrier quartering the reed-beds, and more summer visitors, including several Swallows, Sand Martins and Sedge Warblers, and 10+ Sandwich Terns, resting on Arnold's Marsh. Also 1 Common Sandpiper feeding along the edge of stream at the Quags. Party of 8 Shore Larks here with bright yellow and black faces, and showing small black 'horns'.

Weybourne Camp, Norfolk

Adult Tawny Pipit watched feeding on short turf on top of cliff. Very confiding bird, 'scoped at just a few yards range. Very upright stance, long pale legs and overall pale appearance immediately obvious. Showing rather yellowish face, with broad supercilium, pale buff edges to wing coverts and tertials, and characteristic row of dark spots on closed wing, formed by dark centres to median coverts.

Tawny Pipit. Summer visitor, breeding in most of Europe but not Britain; here it is a rare, though annual, passage migrant, mostly on south and east coasts.

Cley (Daukes' Hide), Norfolk   Evening

Usual stacks of Avocets and Ruff. 18 Black-tailed Godwits, 1 Curlew, 1 Spotted Redshank and 1 Green Sandpiper the only other waders of note. Still 20+ Wigeon and 5 Pintail remaining. One newly-arrived shockingly bright yellow ♂ Yellow Wagtail in pasture just outside hide at dusk.

SE4 ———————————— *April 13* ———— clear, sunny and warm

Weybourne Camp, Norfolk   07.30

Pair of newly-arrived Black Redstarts around old buildings, the ♂ singing with typical stuttering scratchy phrases and sporting fine black plumage with contrasting white wing flashes and orange-red tail. ♀ generally dusky-grey all over with reddish tail.

One pair of Stonechats on bushes. Few migrants except 6 Wheatears and 1 Yellow Wagtail, and 1 late Fieldfare, feeding on grassy slope. Yesterday's adult Tawny Pipit still present, running along disused tarmac tracks, again most confiding.

Black Redstart. A scarce passage migrant, though some birds appear to be virtually resident, breeding regularly in SE England.

Cley, Norfolk   08.25

One adult Osprey sailing east over marshes, loitering high over pools, creating havoc amongst the ducks and waders. Drifted off east along beach, its progress marked by the parties of ducks flushed from the marsh. Upper-parts plain brown, under-parts white with dark carpal patches, and dark mask and mottled 'necklace' noted.

Osprey. Mostly summer visitor to Europe, with a few pairs now nesting in Scotland. A rare but fairly regular passage migrant in England.

[38]

Fine ♀ Marsh Harrier over reserve, also moving east. Dark chocolate brown bird with contrasting golden-yellow crown, throat and leading edge of forewing.

Eight Spotted Redshanks on main pool, including a party of 7 fishing, swimming in deep water, and 45 Golden Plovers, mostly in summer plumage.

Five singing Sedge Warblers, 2 Yellow Wagtails and 2, recently arrived, Willow Warblers, singing in plantation. One Blackcap singing in Walsey Hills, where also 1♂ Brambling perched on top small sapling.

Holkham Pines (West end), Norfolk   11.00

Two recently fledged juvenile Crossbills perched quietly low down in small oaktree beside track, evidence of the early breeding habit of this species.

Few migrants besides several Willow Warblers, Chiffchaffs and 5 Wheatears.

Stiffkey, Norfolk

An early Nightingale singing in disused quarry, a nice bright bird with rufous tail.

Kentish Plover. Scarce passage migrant, mostly in spring.

Cley, Norfolk   14.00

♀ Kentish Plover on Arnold's Marsh. A small, very pale-looking wader with neat breast patches, lacking the definition of head markings of the ♂. Blackish legs and short, quite stout, black bill distinctive.

The same ♀ Hen Harrier as yesterday hunting over the reed-beds, and 4 recently arrived Black Terns hawking around over the main scrape, these in summer dress with black body, grey wings and tail, and white under-tail coverts.

[39]

Black Tern. Summer visitor to Europe; mostly a passage migrant in Britain.

Weybourne Camp, Norfolk

The Tawny Pipit seen again, in flight, calling several times—a fairly soft, dry, rolling 'chrrup'. Also 1 ♂ Ring Ouzel, with scaly black plumage, white crescent across breast, and a little white flecking on crown. Off-yellow base to dark bill noted.

Cley, Norfolk

Similar birds on reserve, but also 20 Sandwich Terns, 1 Whimbrel, 1 Little Stint, and 1 Green Sandpiper. Two House Martins and 1 singing Reed Warbler were also new. One Black Tern flew in from the east, landing on main scrape.

April 15

Apart from 1 or 2 Tree Pipits flying over, no birds of note seen at Southport Golfcourse—least of all the Night Heron. Similarly at Snettisham—very little, besides 1 singing Grasshopper Warbler.

Something of the day was salvaged by seeing the Hoopoe at Broxbourne, Essex—an exotic creature with striking black, white and orangy-pink plumage, watched feeding and flying around grassy area beside rubbish tip, a habitat widespread in Essex.

Four Common Terns over gravel pit, calling.

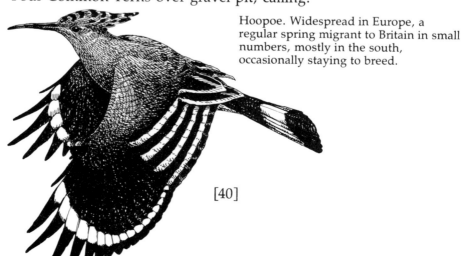

Hoopoe. Widespread in Europe, a regular spring migrant to Britain in small numbers, mostly in the south, occasionally staying to breed.

Salthouse Heath, Norfolk

The Hoopoe flew in across heath in evening, landing on burnt area, where it was most confiding—'scoped at about 30 yards, running around quite rapidly, picking up insects in tip of curved bill and throwing head back to gulp them down. Also seen in bushes and on turf on far side of heath, but relocated later in usual patch. Typically bright orangy, black and white bird, though body looking pale pink in failing light towards dusk.

Hoopoe. Two in two days can't be all bad and nice to see on the home patch.

Cley, Norfolk   15.00

Much the same birds as usual, but waders including flocks of 40, 20 and 10 Bar-tailed Godwits flying east, 6+ Spotted Redshanks, and 12 Knot on Arnold's Marsh. Also about 100 Sandwich and 20 Common Terns, 3 Kittiwakes and 35 Great Black-backed Gulls on here.

The regular Hen Harrier appeared twice over reserve, and 1 Bittern booming during evening.

One Savi's Warbler singing briefly by Daukes' Hide—a distinctive 'wooden' clicking reel.

Cley, Norfolk

The Savi's Warbler watched singing from reeds just outside hide—a surprisingly large and dark warbler, rather rounded tail showing distinct transverse bars. Called once—a hard 'tzwik'.

Savi's Warbler. Having re-established itself as a British breeding species, singing ♂s are now heard at several sites in summer.

A walk around the reserve produced 10+ Spotted Redshanks, in black summer plumage, 15+ Ruff of various colours, 20 Bar-tailed Godwits, and 2 Little Terns.

Other migrants included 2 particularly fine ♂ and 1 ♀ White Wagtails and an early Swift flew west along the beach.

A party of 5 Shore Larks were still in the usual field at the Quags—very vocal, uttering distinctive slurred whistling calls—'tsee seeu'.

A very confiding, full summer-plumaged Lapland Bunting found feeding along edge of the track, on overturned earth and dredged mud. A most handsome bird.

Summer ♂ Lapland Bunting.

White Wagtail. Continental race of Pied Wagtail, chiefly a coastal passage migrant.

One Wryneck seen feeding on turf and sand on Walsey Hills hopping about in pile of dead gorse, often stretching up vertically and peering around. A very boldly marked bird, patterned all over with varied mottling and vermiculations, of grey, buffy-yellow and brown.

Two Sparrowhawks and 1 ♀ Marsh Harrier soaring high overhead, the latter hunting over reed-beds later with upswept wings and dangling bright yellow legs.

One Greenshank feeding on small pool near Pope's Marsh, also 1 black and silver summer-plumaged Grey Plover, along with 3 Whimbrels, on Arnold's Marsh.

Many Yellow Wagtails and Swallows on reserve, and 1 Whitethroat singing from nearby gorse bushes.

Breydon Water, Norfolk 18.30
Hundreds of distant waders and gulls out on mudflats, but little of note except a semi-albino (white-mantled) Black-headed Gull.

Wryneck. Formerly a quite common summer visitor but now a very scarce, but regular, passage migrant.

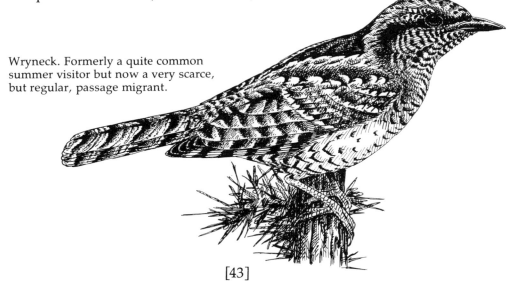

[43]

Thetford, Norfolk   08.30
Four Bar-tailed Godwits flew east over main road.

East Anglia   09.50
Two Goshawks soaring and displaying—'switch backing' and dropping with wings half closed, appearing incredibly big, broad-chested and long-winged compared to a nearby ♀ Sparrowhawk.

Gringley on the Hill, Notts   15.30
Flock of 19 Dotterels scattered in large field of young crops. Later split into groups of 9 and 10, the latter moving close to the road. The majority of birds appeared to be brightly coloured females, with only two dull birds, presumably males. Beautiful and striking birds, but well-concealed when crouching, detectable then only by bold white head-stripe. Piping call heard often from flying birds.

Dotterel. Summer visitor to Scotland in small numbers, 'trips' often appearing at traditional sites in England on spring migration.

Cley, Norfolk   07.30

Ashy-headed Wagtail. One of the Mediterranean forms of Yellow Wagtail, occasionally recorded in Britain.

Migrants on the reserve, apart from the usual waders and terns, included 5 Spotted Redshanks, 3 Whimbrels and 10 Bar-tailed Godwits. Also 1 ♂ Scaup on Snipe's Marsh, and 1 ♀ Marsh Harrier flew out over West Bank.

One ♂ Yellow Wagtail feeding on grassy islands in Carter's Scrape, showing the characteristics of the Ashy-headed race—a very bright bird with blue-grey hood, darkest in front of eye, and clear-cut white throat.

Holkham Pines, Norfolk   12.00

Four Crossbills flying around, calling, and bathing at drinking pool with several Redpolls and 1 ♂ Siskin.

Few new migrants except 2 Lesser Whitethroats, 1 Grasshopper Warbler flushed from tussock grass by track and 1 Wryneck, crawling around in hawthorn bush beside west pool. With its habit of remaining motionless for long periods, and 'dead-wood' camouflage, this bird would seemingly disappear without leaving the bush.

Another Wryneck.

[45]

Cley, Norfolk   14.00

One ♀ Ring Ouzel feeding on village green. Carriage rather horizontal, and sleek compared to Blackbird, with relatively longer wings. Dusky brown plumage with distinct pale scalloping, especially on flanks, pale wing panel and gorget.

Ring Ouzel. Summer visitor, breeding in hilly districts of north and west Britain, and a regular passage migrant elsewhere.

Weybourne Camp, Norfolk

Few migrants except 1 singing Lesser Whitethroat—as always an exceptionally handsome warbler, neatly proportioned with subtle grey, brown and white plumage, highlighted by sharp blackish ear-coverts and legs and delicate pink wash on breast.

   Also another ♀ Ring Ouzel feeding on waste ground and flying with a sharp 'chak chak'.

   One Black Redstart flew across road at Salthouse, landing on roof of pub, a very dusky bird, presumably ♀.

Cley, Norfolk

Similar birds on reserve, including a booming Bittern and 1 ♀ Marsh Harrier jumping about on area of cut reeds, possibly hunting frogs. A pack of about 40 Sandwich and 2 Little Terns were resting on the sand bar on Arnold's Marsh, and 1 Whimbrel flew west at dusk, calling—a most distinctive repeated 'tittering'.

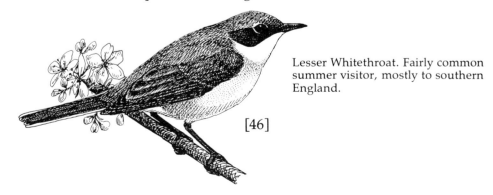

Lesser Whitethroat. Fairly common summer visitor, mostly to southern England.

[46]

Frampton-on-Severn, Glos   06.00
Cuckoo calling at dawn. 1 Whimbrel flew overhead.

Several Yellow Wagtails and Meadow Pipits feeding around muddy shoreline.

The summer-plumaged Red-throated Pipit located feeding on short turf along sea wall. Very confiding bird, allowing excellent views. About size of Meadow Pipit but quite stout-looking, plumage warm brown with quite distinct double wing-bars and pale edges to the tertials, the latter very prominent at some range. Also distinct yellowish lines down either side of mantle. Fairly uniform pinky-brown (brick-coloured) face, throat and chest, merging into bold flank streaks. Pale-based bill and pale legs also noted.

Red-throated Pipit. Summer visitor to Arctic Eurasia, a rare though virtually annual vagrant to Britain in spring or autumn.

Fleet Pond, Hants   10.00
No sign of the reported Blue-winged Teals, or of the Marsh Harrier, which would also have been nice to see on my former patch.

Elvetham Lake, Hants
Two Little Ringed Plovers flew in, calling—characteristic 'pee-u', landing on mud close by. Lack of wing-bar, pale legs and golden-yellow eye-ring noted.

Little Ringed Plover. Formerly a rare vagrant, but now a regular summer visitor, having colonised much of southern Britain.

[47]

Dartford Warbler. A sedentary species, with local distribution in several southern counties.

Two Dartford Warblers singing and calling from gorse bushes on recently recolonised West Surrey heath. Jaunty, long-tailed warbler with clockwork-sounding, rather scratchy song, including whirring call-notes.

Cetti's Warbler. Has colonised suitable habitat in much of southern England since 1971, now seemingly well-established, the first ever recorded in Britain being only ten years earlier.

Stodmarsh, Kent   16.00

One Savi's Warbler singing from sedges beside Lampen Wall, and several Cetti's Warblers singing—typical abrupt explosive phrases. One seen in ditch—very dark rusty brown and buff, with greyish cheeks and breast, whitish supercilium and broad, rounded, dark brown tail.

One ♂ Marsh Harrier watched hunting over reed-beds; presumably not a full adult with the grey on wings partly obscured with brown.

The 2 Glossy Ibis watched circling down to roost-site, the reed-beds west of Lampen Wall. After circling around for some time, one landed, but the other only after its fourth attempt. Both flew up again later and went off high into the sunset. Peculiar prehistoric-looking creatures with blackish plumage, glossed with bronzy-purple and bottle green.

Glossy Ibis. Though with a cosmopolitan
distribution, the nearest colonies are in
SE Europe, and it is a very rare vagrant
to Britain. One of these Kent birds
appears to have arrived in 1975, and is
now a permanent resident.

Dungeness, Kent   08.30

Not surprisingly considering the adverse wind, very little seen on the
sea-watch, apart from a few Commic Terns moving east, 1 Kittiwake, a
small party of Whimbrel and 8 Common Scoter flying eastwards. One
Arctic Skua flew past, low over the sea. A few waders on gravel pits—15
Dunlins, 2 Bar-tailed Godwits, 1 Greenshank, 1 Little Stint and 1 Sanderling. Also 7 Black Terns hawking into the wind over pits, dipping
down to pick food off water surface.

One ♀ Kentish Plover feeding on sand spit, very close to road. Very
pale, dumpy appearance, narrow cheek and breast patches, beady black
eye, dark legs and bill noted.

Kentish Plover. Breeds just across the Channel, but only a rare visitor here.

A search through the bushes produced few migrants other than many Wheatears and Willow Warblers, 1 Cuckoo and 1 Lesser Whitethroat.

A pair of Blue-headed Wagtails running around on gravel beside the Long pits, the male showing typical head pattern—bright blue-grey hood with white supercilium and yellow throat, paler just below cheeks. Female much duller.

One Whinchat on dead thistles beside road, a bright ♂ with dark cheeks bordered above and below by white stripes.

Blue-headed Wagtail. The central European race of Yellow Wagtail, a passage migrant and occasionally breeding in SE England.

[50]

May 7

Abberton Reservoir, Essex

Two visits, in morning and evening, produced no sign of the reported Red-rumped Swallow, resulting in the ultimate depression of dipping.

May 9

Cley, Norfolk   19.00–21.30

A few new waders on the reserve, including 40 Dunlin, 2 'black' Spotted Redshanks, 1 Knot, 4 Common Sandpipers and 1 Wood Sandpiper. One ♂ Scaup again seen on Snipe's Marsh.

Two Short-eared Owls watched flying around over marshes and farmland, perching on hedgerow bushes and glaring around with fierce-looking yellow eyes.

Five Bramblings flew from the plantation in evening, calling—'chuc-chuc', and 'dzee'.

One Barn Owl flew across road near Blakeney at dusk.

The far-carrying reeling song of the Savi's Warbler heard during the night from the reserve.

May 10

Weybourne Camp, Norfolk   05.30

One Nightingale singing from copse.

Whitethroats (10+), 1 Lesser Whitethroat, 1 Stonechat, and 1 Whinchat in bushes. Also several Turtle Doves and Tree Pipits flying over. 1 Hoopoe flew east across the camp, flopping steadily off along the beach. Although appearing to land, it could not be relocated and presumably moved straight through. A quite unexpected bonus bird.

A brief look at Cley produced 3 Wood Sandpipers flying up, calling—an excited triple 'yip yip yip'.

Hoopoe—the third.

[51]

Red-rumped Swallow. Summer visitor to south and east Europe, but rare vagrant to Britain, occurring almost annually in recent years. About 65 have been recorded here.

Abberton Reservoir, Essex   14.45–16.00

At last! One superb Red-rumped Swallow seen immediately on arrival, floating on the wind and hawking around the field beside car park. A real spanker, providing crippling views down to just a few yards, both in flight and perched on nearby fence-wire. Black tail streamers shorter than Swallow's, upper-wings and mantle blackish with blue sheen restricted to mantle and forewings. Body buffish with rufous face and collar, small bluish-black 'set-forward' cap and buff rump with rich orange upper edge. Distinctive black upper- and under-tail coverts also noted. Flight manner much as rather a lethargic House Martin.

Stodmarsh, Kent   18.00–20.30

Several Cetti's Warblers singing, and very good views obtained of a singing Savi's Warbler close to wall. Rather dark in appearance, with rounded tail, thin off-white supercilium, and very long under-tail coverts, reaching nearly to tip of tail.

The same ♂ Marsh Harrier beating into the wind, crossing over the wall, and 1 late ♀ Hen Harrier hunting over reed-beds in evening, the possibility of Montagu's eliminated by heavier build and 'bulging' wing shape.

Few other migrants about apart from several Cuckoos, 2 Common Terns on lake, and 50+ Swifts wheeling overhead.

One Glossy Ibis came in to roost at dusk, circling low over reeds and landing at third attempt.

[52]

Dungeness, Kent   05.00

Fairly good movement of birds east, up-channel: a steady passage of Commic Terns, 1 Roseate Tern, 50+ Kittiwakes, several Fulmars and Gannets, 8 Little Gulls (including 5 adults with black head, dusky under-wing and white upper-wing), 1 Black Tern, 65+ Common Scoters and 55+ Velvet Scoters.

Also 4 Arctic Skuas flew east, and the hoped-for Pomarine Skuas; a party of 8 birds flew past at 05.45. Quite a spectacle, flying in a tight flock, most with characteristic trailing tail 'spoons'. Surprisingly, three were dark-phase birds, and one an intermediate.

Seen later were another 3 Black Terns, an immature Little Gull, a second Roseate Tern (showing very long tail streamers, dark bill and pearl-pink wash on under-parts) and 2 Mediterranean Gulls, in summer plumage (though retaining the sub-adult black wing-tip markings).

Pomarine Skuas, one of the highlights of spring
seabird movements, and Velvet Scoters, which often
pass up-channel in spring in quite large numbers.
Both breed in the Arctic.

Red-rumped Swallow _____ *May 10* _____ Abberton Reservoir, Essex

Red-spotted Bluethroat _____ *May 17* _____ Cley, Norfolk

Roseate Tern. A very local summer visitor, breeding in small numbers mainly in north and west Britain.

Mediterranean Gulls.

May 13

Cley, Norfolk

An influx of waders onto the marsh—relatively high numbers of Ringed Plovers (50+) and Dunlin (90+) as well as 15+ Common Sandpipers, 10+ Bar-tailed Godwits, 10+ Grey Plovers and 1 Golden Plover. Also 3 partial summer-plumaged Curlew Sandpipers and single Greenshank, Little Ringed Plover, Wood Sandpiper, Spotted Redshank and Knot.

Nine or more Little Stints and 3 Temminck's Stints on R.A.R. scrape—the latter obligingly close to hide. Seen to be summer-plumaged birds, far greyer than the Little Stints with some blackish and rufous patterned feathers scattered over upper-parts, especially on scapulars and tertials. White under-parts with greyish breast patches. Distinctive pale legs and white outer tail feathers also noted.

Temminck's Stints. Usually breeds in the Arctic tundra, wintering in the tropics. Here a very scarce passage migrant, chiefly in southern Britain.

Few waterfowl remaining—now only 1 pair each of Pintail and Wigeon, and 10+ Teal.

Amongst the other birds on the reserve, several Ruffs and Black-tailed Godwits were displaying, and several Avocets had young chicks with them. One Marsh Harrier flew east over the reed-beds.

Migrants included several small parties of Turtle Doves moving east-wards, and 1 Tree Pipit feeding along the beach.

Black Terns appeared to be moving along the coastal strip, with at least 34 birds flying east, though 22 by Daukes' Hide were the most present at any one time.

Weybourne Camp, Norfolk

Two singing Nightingales and 1♀ Black Redstart appeared to be the only birds of note present.

[57]

Kelling, Norfolk

One Wood Warbler singing near road in area of birch and oak wood-land. Typically clean-looking bird, rather large with long wings and shortish tail, bright green above with yellow fore-parts and white under-side. Song distinctive—an accelerating, shivering trill and repeated plaintive 'piiu' notes.

Wood Warbler. Widely distributed summer visitor, though rare in places, especially East Anglia.

Spotted Flycatcher. Fairly common summer visitor to most of Britain.

Pied Flycatcher. Summer visitor to much of Wales and northern and west Britain; regular passage migrant on other, coastal areas.

Holkham Pines (West from gap), Norfolk

Summer visitors much in evidence with several Cuckoos, Blackcaps, Lesser Whitethroats and Garden Warbler.

One ♀ Redstart flitting along path—greyish-brown bird, paler below, with bright orangy-rufous tail, constantly quivering.

One Spotted Flycatcher in pinetrees beside pool, 1 ♂ and 1 ♀ Pied Flycatcher feeding separately beside main track, the startling black and white ♂ looking rather out of place in the fresh-leaved poplar trees.

One Firecrest, singing—surprisingly distinctive, accelerating string of 'zeeta' notes usually lacking the terminal flourish of the Goldcrest.

Holkham Hall Lake, Norfolk

Flock of 14 Black Terns and 1 Arctic Tern swooping around at top end of pool. The stout, blood-red bill of the Arctic noticeable at some range—perhaps the only fully reliable field point.

Titchwell, Norfolk

Another 18 Black Terns, feeding over flooded scrape, 3 birds perched on posts. Two Common Sandpipers and 2 Wood Sandpipers on grassy islands. Two ♂ Marsh Harriers flying together over far side of reserve.

One ♂ Garganey seen feeding amongst floating vegetation, and flying across to sea pools. Unmistakable with rich brown and white coloration, white head-stripes, and pale blue-grey fore-wing in flight.

Cley, Norfolk

One White Wagtail on Carter's Scrape.

Over 160 Sandwich, 10 Little and 20 Common Terns resting on Arnold's Marsh in evening.

Garganey. Regular, though scarce, summer visitor.

NE1 ———————— *May 15* ———————— sunny

Cley, Norfolk   18.15–20.30

One ♂ Ortolan hopping around on gravel and grass at far end of track opposite Billy's Hide. Rather distant, but typical jizz with olive-grey head and chest, yellow throat and moustachials, and orange under-parts quite obvious. Warm brown streaked upper-parts, pale edgings to wing feathers, white on outer tail feathers and pale pinkish bill also noted, but eye-ring not visible at range.

Ortolan Bunting. Widespread in Europe; in Britain a rare annual drift migrant in spring and autumn.

One Red-necked Phalarope on small pool in marshy area near road, feeding with usual nervous jerky action, also 'spinning'. Reasonably bright, summer-plumaged bird, probably a female. Slaty-grey head and breast, extending as smudgy lines on flanks, with quite extensive rusty-red patch on either side of neck. Dark upper-parts with several yellowy-buff stripes. White under-parts, chin and eye-spot noted, and extremely fine black bill.

Red-necked Phalarope. Mostly a scarce passage migrant, though does breed in small numbers in Scotland. Fairly regularly seen in Norfolk in spring.

Also in view from the road were 1 Wood Sandpiper, and 2+ Temminck's Stints on muddy islands in Carter's Scrape, and many Black Terns hawking, with a party of 18 in front of Daukes' Hide later.

Waders visible from this hide included 150+ Dunlin, 12+ Common Sandpipers, 10+ Bar-tailed Godwits (including one particularly red summer-plumaged bird), 14 Little Stints and 3 Curlew Sandpipers, as well as 1 Greenshank, 1 Spotted Redshank and above-average number of Ringed Plovers.

Of about 20 Ruff present, several males had variously-coloured ruffs and ear tufts, two birds displaying on close island.

A few Pintails and Teal, 1 Lesser Whitethroat singing, and several Cuckoos. Parties of waders moving off east during the evening.

Cley and Weybourne Camp, Norfolk   05.45–07.30

Noticeably far fewer waders than yesterday, with no sign of the Phalarope, but the Ortolan was still present, hopping around closer to the road.

A few Black-tailed Godwits, 6+ Little Stints and 1 Greenshank noted here, and only a few Whitethroats and Wheatears at the camp.

Bluethroat. The red-spotted race, which breeds in Scandinavia, occurs regularly in small numbers here in the autumn and rarely in the spring.

Cley, Norfolk   14.15

A crippling ♂ Red-spotted Bluethroat watched in bright sunshine beside North Hide, a very confiding bird apparently totally unaware of its audience and feeding within a few feet, on an area of sand and turf dotted with gorse and nettle patches. Sporting a shining satin-blue gorget bordered by black, with a chestnut-red central patch and a mottled band of rufous below. Upper-parts a curious steely-grey/brown and under-parts off-white, showing strong buffy-white supercilia, and some red just discernible on sides of tail.

One Bittern flew across the reserve, landing in field by coastguards.

Titchwell, Norfolk   16.00

Five Black Terns and 1 immature Little Gull flying over freshwater scrape, and 2 Little Stints feeding out on the saltings.

At least 1 pair of Marsh Harriers, seen both over the reed-beds and, later, over the adjacent farmland.

One ♂ Montagu's Harrier seen flying over fields on hilltop, showing typical rakish silhouette, lacking the broadness across the secondaries of Hen Harrier, darker grey plumage (with a 'hooded' appearance), and no white on rump.

[61]

Cley, Norfolk   06.30

A variety of waders included several Ruff, 60+ Dunlin, 6 Little Stints, 1 Wood Sandpiper and 3 partial summer-plumaged Curlew Sandpipers, but the only other birds of note were 1 ♀ Marsh Harrier, 1 Whinchat, and 1 Bittern which flew twice over the reed-beds.

Titchwell, Norfolk   18.00

The ♂ Montagu's Harrier came in over poplars, flying over close corner of reed-beds. Landed in reeds, but flew back up to fields later. Seen to be dark grey above, darker on forewings and hood, with black primaries and wing-bars on upper-wing, heavy barring on under-wing, and with quite extensive rusty streaking on flanks. Also seen here were 3+ Marsh Harriers, and 1 late Fieldfare.

Pair of Marsh Harriers. Mainly summer visitor, breeding in small, but increasing, numbers in East Anglia.

Montagu's Harrier. Summer visitor. Britain's rarest breeding bird of prey.

Little Owl. Resident, introduced in the 19th century, now widespread and relatively common.

Holme, Norfolk
One ♀ Ring Ouzel seen on fencepost, and flying across paddocks.

Two Little Owls seen on the journey home, at Stradsett and North-wold, the second perched rather precariously on roadside wires.

================================*May 19*================== dark

Dummer, Near Basingstoke, Hants 03.00–05.00
The Scops Owl heard soon after arrival, singing from horse-chestnut trees near the church. Distinctive, monotonous song—a soft bell-like muffled whistle 'pew . . . . . . pew . . . . . pew . . . . . .' occasionally varying very slightly in pitch and quite ventriloquial, repeated constantly at $2–2\frac{1}{2}$ second intervals. Seen only poorly in trees and flying.

Though this bird stayed most of the summer, to the delight of hundreds of birdwatchers (and the media), it would appear that its presence was initially suppressed, even by some birdwatchers who would waste little time getting to other rarities. The fashionable trend of unreasonable suppression is a habit abhorrent to most birders.

Calm ================================*May 20*================== cloudy

Minsmere, Suffolk 19.15–21.00
No sign of the reported white-winged Black Tern, but some of the regular birds seen, including Marsh Harrier and Avocets. Also 1 Little Gull, while 1 Grasshopper Warbler, 1 Savi's Warbler and 1 Cetti's Warbler were heard singing from the reserve.

[63]

Black-winged Stilt. Summer visitor to
Europe, but a very rare vagrant to
Britain, mostly in the south.

Hickling Broad, Norfolk

The Black-winged Stilt seen standing at back of large scrape in reed-beds, preening. Also watched feeding, rather lethargically, in shallow water. Appeared particularly ungainly with incredibly long wax-pink legs, seemingly having to put much effort into reaching down to water surface. Neat black and white plumage with quite extensive black smudging on crown, down the nape and on 'shoulders'—presumably a male.

[64]

Spoonbill. An annual visitor in very small numbers, most often to East Anglia and the south coast, and usually in summer.

Cley, Norfolk
One Spoonbill feeding in ditch in front of North Hide. Though spending much of its time asleep, occasionally feeding with typical sweeping filter action in quite deep water. Apparently an adult, with long spatulate, yellow-tipped, black bill and lumpy crest, otherwise pure white plumage, black legs.

Later in the day, the Quail at Cromer failed to perform as did the reported White-winged Black Tern at Sizewell, indeed, few other birds seen at all, much of the day being lost to hitching between sites, tickers' car being at Aberdeen!

Great Reed Warbler. A summer visitor, widespread in Europe, occurring as a vagrant in Britain, though annually in recent years as an overshoot, mainly to SE England.

Fleet Pond, Hants

The Great Reed Warbler performing excellently in the evening, singing virtually all the time from topmost reed-heads—a distinctive, loud, unmusical collection of croaking, gurking and piping notes in short repeated phrases. Occasionally flew between reed-beds and perched in alder bushes, calling—a far-carrying 'grrrk'.

Huge in comparison with the Reed Warblers nearby, appearing virtually thrush-sized. Plumage fairly uniform—warm brown above, with darker crown, primaries and centres to secondaries and wing coverts, off-white below with clouded creamy-brown on flanks and face. Strong dark line from bill through eye and creamy supercilia to just behind eye. Long, rather stout bill, brown, with flesh-coloured base and lower mandible, brown legs and hazel irides.

The most striking and stunning feature was the bright orange-red inside of the gape, contrasting with the silky-white puffed throat.

[66]

Dummer, Hants 21.30

The Scops Owl again heard calling continuously from the roadside trees in the village; again proving impossible to see, but audible from the pub!

May 28

Fleet Pond, Hants

The Great Reed Warbler was again performing most satisfactorily, shouting from its favoured perch in the phragmites bed—'scoped from above, straight into huge red gape!

Breydon Water, Great Yarmouth, Norfolk 18.30–21.00

With the waders being pushed up onto exposed mud by the rising tide, 60+ Ringed Plovers, 25+ Dunlin, 2 full summer-plumaged Curlew Sandpipers, 1 Greenshank and 1 Whimbrel appeared, and the Broad-billed Sandpiper was located quite easily. Though first seen at some distance, the bird was gradually forced, by the tide, to move onto the edge of the saltings, where it could be watched at closer range.

Recognisable at distance by 'hunched' stance and very dark upper-parts contrasting with white belly. Seen to be slightly smaller and neater than the accompanying Dunlins, with shorter legs giving it a rather low, 'flat' look. Longish bill quite straight, kinked downwards at tip. Strong pale 'v' patterning on mantle, pale edged wing coverts and split supercilia noted at closer range. Perhaps reminiscent of Purple Sandpiper in flight, appearing very dark overall.

Few other birds seen during the evening besides 2 Great Crested Grebes in the main channel, and 2 Flamingos flying around, providing a touch of the ridiculous.

Broad-billed Sandpiper. Breeding in northern Eurasia and wintering in the Mediterranean and SW Asia, it is a rare vagrant to Britain. Sixty-three have been recorded here, mostly in autumn, but recently has occurred several times in spring, in East Anglia.

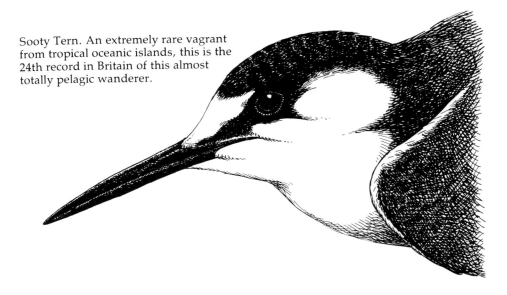

Sooty Tern. An extremely rare vagrant from tropical oceanic islands, this is the 24th record in Britain of this almost totally pelagic wanderer.

Higham Ferrers Gravel-pits, Northants   03.45–06.00

About 60 Black-headed Gulls on islands at dawn. Also a few Gadwall and Teal, and 3 Dunlin.

The Sooty Tern appeared at the edge of muddy island, flopping about pathetically with half-open wings. Obviously an extremely sick bird, nevertheless a total 'blocker' for those who saw it before it was rescued from its unfortunate situation. Very striking bird—a large tern with white forehead, face and under-parts. Crown, and line through eye to bill, black with slight buff feather edgings. White-edged forked tail noted and under-wings seen to be white with dark flight feathers. Long, strong bill black in colour, legs and feet grey.

After some time it became clear that this bird would not survive in this sorry state, so it was picked up, calling aggressively, and taken to a bird-hospital, and then to become a national celebrity. Despite apparently regaining its strength, it was not released into the wild as was hoped, and did eventually die in captivity.

June 7

Cley, Norfolk

Very few birds of interest on the reserve apart from 3 Little Stints, seen from Daukes' Hide.

Weybourne Camp, Norfolk

One Dotterel running around on area of rough grass and weeds on the seaward edge of the camp. A ridiculously tame creature, feeding unperturbed within 3 yards of us. An excellent bird, but possibly not as bright as some. Presumably a male, with rather mottled face-markings and upper-parts noted, and rather untidy orange and black belly.

Flew up, calling—a woody 'prrerp', circled around offshore and landed a little further along beach.

Cley, Norfolk

One Bittern booming most of the day; one flew out over West Bank. The same 3 Little Stints on Pat's Pool, also 4 late Dunlins, 1 Greenshank, 1 Bar-tailed Godwit, 1 Turnstone and 1 Grey Plover. Several Oystercatchers and Redshanks with chicks, and stacks of very noisy, belligerent Avocets with young at all stages of growth.

Other birds on the reserve included 20 Teal, 5 Shovelers, several juvenile Bearded Tits and 3–4 second-year Little Gulls—these, though presumably the same age, showing varying amounts of immature plumage, with one bird sporting a black hood as well as the dusky wing-bars.

Dotterel. Presumably a late migrant or non-breeder, this bird showed an almost stupid tameness, a feature common to the species in general.

[69]

Bittern. Resident and winter visitor, its breeding stronghold appears to be East Anglia with others in Lancashire and Kent.

June 12

East Tilbury Gravel Pits, Essex   11.00–13.30

Exhaustive flogging of the area produced no sign of the Little Egret, which had presumably chosen this time to visit Cliffe Marshes, across the Thames—a particularly annoying habit of this summering individual. Very few other birds of any kind seen besides the usual Yellow Wagtails, Shelducks and Common Terns, though a party of 26 Grey Herons flying around together over Mucking Pits was quite impressive.

Great Wakering, Essex   14.00

One Black-winged Stilt, located immediately, standing on one leg, preening, in nearest pool to road. Quite confiding bird, it soon began feeding along the near edge of pool, allowing crippling views. Usual very sharp black and white plumage, with quite extensive black head-markings, these extending down nape and narrowing on 'shoulders'. Also very fine black bill (perhaps very slightly upturned), ridiculously long pink legs and projecting primaries noted. At such close range, a subtle peachy wash was visible on the breast, as was the bright red eye and grey tail.

Black-winged Stilt. Though several were recorded in 1980, it seems likely that this could be the same individual previously seen at Hickling.

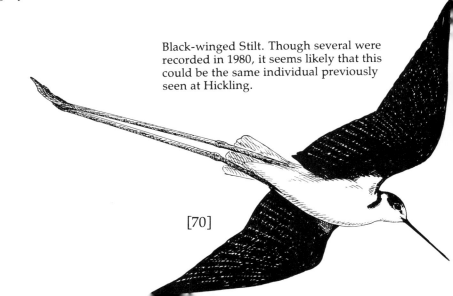

[70]

After feeding for some time, the bird flew up to join a group of shrieking Redshanks, disappearing with them towards the saltings. A stroll around the sea wall produced a plethora of Corn Buntings and Yellow Wagtails, 1 female Wigeon, and 6+ Avocets, the latter very vocal and seen feeding on both the fresh pools and tidal mud-banks.

Later, the Black-winged Stilt flew over, high over fields—picked up on scraping, tern-like, call. Seen to land in tidal channel, where it stayed only briefly before flying out onto Potton Island. An amazing creature in flight with white rump extending well up back, long trailing legs and seemingly independent primary tips.

SW4 _____*June 14*_____ intermittent rain

The Brecks, Norfolk

One Kingfisher flew along canal.

Pair of Red-backed Shrikes watched at a traditional site. The ♂ seen first, busily preening immediately after thunderstorm, then ♀ appeared in the bushes. ♂ in immaculate plumage, as usual, with dove-grey hood, rufous mantle and black mask and tail, latter rather rounded and showing white panels at base. White under-parts washed with a delicate pink colouring. The ♀ rather dull, brownish above and pale below, but this individual showing a dark mask and heavily blotched breast.

Red-backed Shrikes. Passage migrant and summer visitor, rapidly decreasing in numbers and seemingly on the verge of extinction as a breeding bird in Britain.

Woodlark. Locally distributed as a breeding bird mostly in southern Britain, it seems to benefit from modern forestry techniques, often colonising temporarily cleared areas.

About 3 pairs of Woodlarks around clearing in pine forest, with 2–3 ♂s singing over area of young pines. One bird 'scoped, singing from fencewire, and several birds seen well feeding amongst heather and bracken. Distinctive both in flight, with broad wings and short tail, and on the deck, with neatly patterned plumage, broad creamy supercilia meeting at nape and characteristic black and white carpal patch. Several birds calling, both on the ground and flying—a liquid 'tloolooeet', this call often introduced into rather musical, mellow song, uttered in short phrases from fluttering circular song-flight, and often sounding peculiarly distant despite the bird being relatively close.

Stone-curlew. Summer visitor, breeding in small numbers on suitable heath and downland habitat in SE England.

Five Stone-curlews out on area of rabbit-grazed turf: a pair with two well-grown young and a third adult, this bird apparently causing some aggravation by being present and eliciting a clamouring response from the other adults. Surprisingly well-camouflaged birds, being basically streaked brown and buff, but with rather reptilian features—stary yellow eyes, similarly coloured legs and (black-tipped) bill. Exhibiting unique wing-pattern, of double white bars on mid-wing and white patches on inner primaries and leading edge, when flying in to feed the young birds with worms. The juveniles appeared as smaller, untidy versions of the adults, but with greeny-based bill.

Worcester   17.00
Several Reed and Sedge Warblers, and 1 Lesser Whitethroat, singing between showers. Many Cuckoos, in good voice, including 2 birds indulging in display antics, tails high and wings drooped, and gurgling incoherently.

Marsh Warbler. A scarce summer visitor, regularly breeding in only very small numbers at a few traditional sites.

About 3 Marsh Warblers located singing from a marshy area, one of the traditional sites. Though two of the rival males included completely different phrases, the lively varied song, lacking much of the harsher notes typical of the other Acros and indeed seemingly totally mimetic, was quite distinctive, even at some distance.

Close views were obtained of only one of these birds—though basically similar to Reed Warbler, looking far greyer, especially about the head and upper mantle. Wings and tail plain brownish, lacking any hint of rufous, under-parts off-white and distinctly pale straw-coloured legs. Inside to gape noted as quite pale orange.

Dummer, Hants
No sight or sound of the Scops Owl, probably due to the bad weather.

[73]

Bricksbury, Hants   09.00

Few birds, but those seen quite distinctive of the heath-edge habitat—1 Woodlark, 1 Redstart and several Tree Pipits singing, and Green Woodpeckers feeding on ants on the turf.

Green Woodpecker. Rather common resident, more often heard than seen.

Redstart. Widely distributed summer visitor, with locally fluctuating populations.

Tree Pipit. Summer visitor, common on suitable heathlands and areas with scattered trees or other convenient songposts.

Little Egret. Breeds in southern Europe.
A rare vagrant to Britain, though
occurring annually in small numbers in
recent years, mainly in early summer.

East Tilbury Gravel Pits, Essex 13.30

Second time lucky. The adult Little Egret seen with no trouble at the gravel pits, mostly standing on one leg on sand bar. Watched preening meticulously, retaining the hunched pose, often fluffing out the fine mass of plumes on back and chest (though seeming to lack the elongated crest plumes).

Plumage pure white, but apparently in breeding colours with dark-tipped blue bill (showing greener at base with flesh-coloured area up to bright yellow eye) and black legs with orangy-yellow feet.

Spent some time fishing, when presenting a very different shape—a very streamlined, elegant bird. Dashed energetically around pit edges, often in quite deep water, stabbing at and swallowing many small fish in quick succession.

[75]

Sizewell Power Station, Suffolk   20.30–21.30

After a hectic scorch across East Anglia, the Woodchat Shrike was located quite quickly, perched on top of a pile of dead wood inside the boundary fence. It soon came onto the close bushes, from where it hunted by dropping down onto insects in the grass. A very striking, brightly coloured bird, probably a male.

Basically black and white plumage—black face mask, mantle, wings and tail, with large white scapular patches, white rump and white under-parts, relieved by a rich rufous hood. Also showing a small white patch at base of black bill, dark eye and grey feet. White patch at base of primaries and white edged tail obvious in flight.

The bird later returned to the heap of dead wood, disappearing into this, presumably to roost.

One Stonechat and several Wheatears around the wasteground, and 1 particularly fine ♂ Black Redstart singing from the power station buildings.

Also 20+ Little Terns fishing around the 'patch' (the warm water outfall from the power station), and 1 Little Owl perched on top of telegraph pole beside road on journey home.

Woodchat Shrike. A summer visitor to south and central Europe, a few occurring virtually annually in Britain, as either spring overshoots or autumn wanderers.

The Brecks, Norfolk

Another visit to the 'pine-trees', inspired by rumours of a Two-barred Crossbill, resulted in a fruitless search of the area. However, a Woodlark taking food to its young provided a pleasant diversion.

Nightjar. A summer visitor,
crepuscular in habit and apparently
decreasing in numbers, found in suitable
woodland clearings, young plantations
and heathland habitat.

Two or three Nightjars began 'churring' at dusk from an area of cleared pine-forest—a rather mechanical, sustained dry purring, occasionally changing in pitch giving a weird ventriloquial quality. One male, with its subtle 'dead-leaf' camouflaged plumage relieved by large white spots on wings and tail, seen flying over clearing with typical buoyant flight, interspersed with glides, the wings held in a 'v' shape.

Another bird seen in half-light perched lengthways along a spindly branch and flying after a moth with surprising agility for such an apparently unco-ordinated creature. Heard calling—a liquid 'goo-ik'.

The Brecks, Suffolk

♂ Red-backed Shrike watched hunting from dead trees and wires around wasteland near factory, often diving into bushes, a tactic apparently designed to disturb possible prey, and seemingly successful, the bird often chasing out to catch flying insects.

Cley, Norfolk   09.00–16.30

Most birds on the reserve now with young at all stages of development. The Avocets, Lapwings, Canada and Greylag Geese all seemed to be particularly successful, as were the Ringed Plovers, Redshanks, Oyster-catchers, Mallard and Shelduck.

Spotted Redshank and Greenshank, both in summer plumage. These birds, though basically migrants and seen in some numbers in spring and autumn, are often present in summer and, more rarely, in winter.

Parties of Lapwings seen flying west along the coast through the day—presumably a post-breeding dispersive movement, as with the Starlings, also flying west in quite large flocks. Other migrants included 2+ summer-plumaged Spotted Redshanks and 1 Greenshank, and about 150 Swifts—these shifting around the coast between the showers.

A party of juvenile Bearded Tits watched from Bittern Hide, grovelling about on the mud at base of reeds, looking very orange, heavily marked with black stripes—theoretically as an adaptation to their skulking reed-bed existence.

One Blue-headed type Wagtail put in a brief appearance on R.A.R. Scrape, while a party of 7 Egyptian Geese, a white and ginger-coloured Ruff, and 1 Gannet (flying offshore) were also noted.

Over 20 Kestrels seen from car on journey to Cornwall, and 3+ Buzzards beside the road in Devon.

Hayle Estuary, Cornwall   19.15

With the ebbing tide, 40+ Curlews and many gulls began appearing on the exposed mudbanks.

The Laughing Gull arrived on cue, flying over Copperhouse Creek, but then off towards the sea. Seen to be about Common Gull size, with long wings and drooping bill, dark grey mantle and wings, merging into black wing-tips. Also showing white trailing edge to wing and dark hood.

Though 'tickable', not really a very satisfactory performance, and after an hour the bird obligingly re-appeared, and could then be thoroughly grilled. Very confiding, it spent the evening running back and forth on exposed mud, eating many small crabs. Seen to be little bigger than Black-headed Gull, but much longer-winged and more sturdily built. Not quite in full summer plumage, with brownish wing coverts showing on otherwise dark grey upper-parts, and incomplete dark ashy-grey/brown hood. Very long, stout dark red bill, and longish reddish legs.

Laughing Gull, North America. Only the 23rd bird ever to be recorded in Britain, but several have been seen in recent years.

South Coast

One Quail calling from cornfields on headland, heard intermittently from 02.30—the characteristic repeated liquid 'quit-quit-it' of the male audible at some range.

A sea-watch from soon after dawn produced a large gathering of Gannets offshore, fishing in a tight wheeling group over area of choppy sea. 500+ birds present at any one time, but more birds commuting back and forth to the west, presumably from nearest breeding colonies.

Local seabirds included several Guillemots and Razorbills, and at least three Puffins flying offshore, as well as the usual Shags, Fulmars and Kittiwakes.

Five Manx Shearwaters flew past, 3 west just offshore and 2 east further out, showing typical sharply contrasted black and white plumage, but having to abandon the usual free 'shearing' flight action and flap in the calm conditions.

Unusually for the time of year, 1 light-phase Arctic Skua flew steadily past eastwards, and 4 Common Scoter also flew east.

Manx Shearwater. A summer visitor, birds seen on the south coast in summer are likely to be on feeding flights from the west-coast colonies.

Rock Pipit. Resident around the coastline of Britain, but breeding only sparingly away from the west and north.

[80]

Several Rock Pipits singing and feeding along clifftop. Very dusky birds, a little bulkier than Meadow Pipit, with little definition to the plumage apart from a reasonably distinct eye-ring. Outer tail feathers characteristically smoky-grey.

Few other birds seen besides 1 ♀ Sparrowhawk hunting low across fields, flushing many Linnets and Corn Buntings, but catching none.

One Cetti's Warbler heard singing from reed-beds nearby, beside footpath.

One ♂ Montagu's Harrier watched gliding around in valley, and flying into fields of crops near main road with prey, to be received by a female, which took the prey item to the young. The male, a very clean-plumaged bird with neat black wing-tips and wing-bars, also showing heavy rusty streaking on under-parts, especially on flanks, spent much of the time circling lazily over valley, while the female (dark brown, narrow-winged with small white rump patch) appeared only the once.

Three Buzzards soaring over woodland on typically broad, up-turned wings. Very bulky, round-headed raptors.

Montagu's Harrier.

Two Dartford Warblers on bracken and small birches on ridge, 1 singing. Distinctively small warbler with long tail, dark grey brown above and dull vinous below, with reddish eye and eye-ring, orangy legs.

Two or three Honey Buzzards seen several times during the afternoon. Often two birds soaring together, one displaying by banking up and 'wing-clapping', fluttering the wings while held stiffly above body in deep 'v'. Wings characteristically held level with body while soaring, and slightly down-curved when gliding, unlike Buzzard. In silhouette showing quite long wings with 'pinched-in' bases, quite long tail and distinctive smallish, projecting head.

Other birds in the area included breeding Curlews, Redshanks and Snipe on marshy ground, several of the latter 'drumming' in evening, several Stonechats and 1 migrant Green Sandpiper.

Honey Buzzard. Recorded in Britain as an irregular passage migrant, and breeding regularly in very small numbers in the south.

Dummer, Hants   22.00

The Scops Owl calling continuously for ¼ hour from trees in village gardens, though only tantalising views obtained of the bird, in curious, wavering (Woodcock-like) flight.

[82]

Dummer, Hants   21.30–22.00

Scored at last! On the fifth visit, crippling views of the Scops Owl, perched on edge of hole in tree-trunk close to road. Watched here for about 20 minutes, spotlighted by car headlights, and seen to be a small, intricately patterned grey-brown owl with extended ear-tufts and penetrating yellow eyes set in dark centred facial discs, the latter also edged with a blackish line. After staring at us, apparently fascinated by the curious twitching antics (including dismembering a colleague's car to arrange the lighting), for 20 minutes, it flew up into branches of tree, perching on a small branch, then off into the gardens and commenced calling.

Scops Owl. Summer visitor to southern Europe, very rare north of its breeding range, this summering individual became a national celebrity, and was the first twitchable occurrence of this species.

Irvine Harbour, Ayrshire 19.50–20.30

The sub-adult Franklin's Gull flew in to bathe in tidal creek, allowing close views both on the deck and flying. At rest, appeared to be in virtually adult plumage—grey mantle, slightly darker than Common Gull (but a shade paler than Laughing Gull!), with broad white tips to secondaries showing as a white band, and black hood, incomplete on throat and lores, with prominent broken white eye-ring. Dark red bill and reddish legs.

In flight showing several immature characteristics, but in heavy wing-moult, lacking some inner primaries and a patch of white showing near base of primaries. Wings above showing dark brown primaries and subterminal band across secondaries, but below, all-white. Tail white with broad grey band down centre. Though slightly smaller than the nearby Black-headed Gulls, more stoutly built with the wings surprisingly broad for shortish length. Few other birds seen during the evening except 15 Golden Plovers on newly exposed mud, several Eiders, and 250 Lesser Black-backed Gulls in a nearby stubble field.

Franklin's Gull. There have only been six records of this North American gull, all since 1970.

Lake District   08.45–09.30

Pair of Golden Eagles watched flying and soaring around rocky ridge of hill, as well as perched on boulders for some time. Very impressive birds in the air with long, broad wings, longish tail and projecting head and bill. The female appeared huge, dark chocolate-brown all over with golden hood, showing a little white at base of primaries and tail. The male much smaller and paler overall, with quite extensive pale straw-coloured hood and larger pale buff patches on upper-wings. Also showing slightly more white on tail and flight feathers than ♀.

One Ring Ouzel heard calling from scree-slopes in valley.

One Yellow Wagtail feeding a juvenile on bracken-covered hilltop above lake—a rather strange encounter, this species generally preferring lowland marshes.

Three Buzzards over hillsides, including one bird flying steadily alongside the car at up to 30 m.p.h.!

Golden Eagle. Though well distributed in Scotland, especially in the west, a very rare bird in Britain.

Two Redstarts flew up from the roadside, and 1 Merlin seen from car on Shap Fell, shifting low across the fields.

Titchwell, Norfolk   19.10

One summer-plumaged adult Gull-billed Tern watched from hide, patrolling the tern-colony on shingle beach and resting with gulls on the mud, often within a few yards of the hide. A relatively large tern, rather broad-winged and 'bull-necked' in flight, with shallowly forked tail. Plumage uniform soft grey above, on mantle, wings, rump and tail, the latter with slightly paler edges, and the primaries edged and tipped darker. White below. Neatly proportioned, quite rounded head with neat black cap, and short, stout, all-black bill. Also showed relatively long, black legs.

The bird spent much of its time flying around, with quite gull-like, shallow wing-beats, scrounging any unguarded scraps of food from the Little Tern colony, even from the bills of young terns, apparently annoying some adult Common Terns, which often mobbed it.

Gull-billed Tern. Breeds in various areas of Europe, the closest colony being perhaps in Denmark, but occurs in Britain only as a vagrant, chiefly in spring.

Other birds on the reserve included 10+ sub-adult Little Gulls on the large flooded area, busily picking food from the floating vegetation and water surface, and 1 Black Tern hawking over the same area.

Also a vast wheeling mass of Swifts and Swallows had gathered, feeding over the reserve, presumably attracted by the profusion of midges.

One Grasshopper Warbler heard singing from car-park—typical sustained 'fishing-reel' trill.

Wandlebury Monument, Cambridge

The Icterine Warbler watched singing from exposed branch in tall ash sapling beside car park. Though moving around and singing from various trees, it seemed keen to return to this favoured perch.

Rather distinctive song perhaps similar in style to Marsh Warbler, containing much mimicry, though quite repetitious in character and generally quite strident, including standard phrases and various discordant notes.

Not a particularly bright bird, being generally olivy grey-brown above and off-white to buff below, though quite yellow on throat, and yellowish on breast and face, with a short supercilium and pale panel on closed wing.

Structurally a rather bulky warbler with quite long wings and peaked crown, with steep forehead and heavy bill typical of the hippo (*Hippolais* warblers). Small black eye, brownish legs, grey feet and dark-tipped pinky-orange bill also noted.

Icterine Warbler. A rare passage migrant, mostly in autumn.

One Lesser Spotted Woodpecker heard calling from oak trees beyond clearing—a repeated shrill 'pee-pee-pee ...' And a Great Spotted Woodpecker seen.

No sign of a reported Hoopoe at Wixoe, nor of the Sabine's Gull at Sheringham, a look at the rough sea here producing only several Kittiwakes, Gannets, and Bar-tailed Godwits flying west, and 1 Manx Shearwater also moving west, off Cley.

[87]

Sheringham sea-front, Norfolk   17.15–19.20

Many Fulmars, 10+ Kittiwakes and 10+ Gannets, flying both east and west offshore.

Five Manx Shearwaters flew past, 5 Bar-tailed Godwits and 2♀ Red-breasted Mergansers also moving west, these rather unusual birds to see off this coast in summer.

At 18.30 the Sabine's Gull flew in, from the west, to feed around the sewage outfall, about 200 yards offshore, with several Black-headed Gulls, then remaining in the vicinity of the pink marker buoy for 40 minutes.

Flight (into the wind and thus remaining in the same area), quite easy and buoyant, often fluttering low over the waves, occasionally hidden from view in the troughs. A very graceful gull, with long, pointed wings and forked tail, in virtually full summer plumage. Hyper-distinctive wing-pattern of clear-cut grey, white and black triangles, incomplete dark grey hood with black border around the neck and shortish, yellow-tipped, black bill noted.

Sabine's Gull. A Nearctic tundra-breeder, pelagic in winter. In Britain a scarce visitor, mainly in autumn, and very rarely recorded in summer.

Skye, Hebrides   06.00

A total of 42 Hooded Crows and 2 Ravens seen at roadside across the island.

One Corncrake flew across the road, apparently trying to land on a cottage windowsill! Typically rail-like in flight with broad wings, short rounded tail, projecting head and neck, and trailing legs. Plumage generally buffish, marked darker brown, with rich rufous wings and contrasting blackish-centred tertials. Pale face, blue-grey wash on neck, conical pink bill and yellowish/flesh-coloured legs noted.

Heard calling from area of sedges—a most characteristic double rasping note, loud and persistent.

Corncrake. A fast declining summer-visitor, which though still apparently fairly numerous in Ireland, retains only a tenuous foothold in Britain, mostly in western Scotland.

Ferry crossing, Uig to Tarbert   09.15–11.30

Five or more Black Guillemots on sea and flying, just out from the harbour. Unmistakable, small auks with uniform black plumage except for large white oval patch on wings, and red feet. Also many Razorbills and Guillemots, and many Puffins floating in small rafts, or flying in parties of up to 20 birds, adding their unique quality to the proceedings.

Black Guillemot. Resident, breeding quite commonly along the north and west coasts of Scotland and the islands, but rare elsewhere.

Sooty Shearwater. Breeding in the southern oceans, this world-wanderer 'winters' in the North Atlantic. Regularly seen off the west coast in autumn, these birds are probably on their way back to breed on the Falklands or Tierra del Fuego in the southern summer.

Manx Shearwaters (12+) seen from boat, and 6+ Storm Petrels flying low over the waves with characteristic wavering action, showing white rump and square tail.

One Sooty Shearwater watched flying close alongside boat—a fairly large shearwater with relatively heavy body and narrow wings. Plumage dark brown all over, relieved only by suffused pale grey underwing-linings.

One Great Skua loitering behind the boat with a few Herring Gulls, occasionally dropping down onto the water, but soon catching up with boat. Typically all-dark skua, flecked liberally with buffy markings and very prominent white wing flashes.

Great Skua. Mostly a summer visitor, breeding in colonies in Shetlands, also in the Orkneys and western Scotland. A passage migrant on other coasts.

[90]

Leucistic Herring Gull, a colour mutant lacking feather pigmentation but retaining the soft-part colouring.

One very small, blue-backed, Merlin flew across bay, low over sea, with typical fast jinking flight on flickering wings.

More of the various seabirds seen from the boat, including several parties of Gannets moving south, and 150 Manx Shearwaters, mostly in small groups but a party of 24, and one of 50 birds, apparently feeding by plunging shallowly into the water.

One leucistic Herring Gull following the boat, with pure white plumage but showing the yellow and red bill, yellow eye and pink legs typical of the normal adult bird.

Many Fulmars seen, including 1 dusky-plumaged 'blue'-phase individual.

Dark-phase Fulmar. Though a common colour variation in the northern parts of its range, these 'blue' birds are quite rare in British waters.

Four summer plumaged Red-throated Divers flew over Lochmaddy Harbour, and 2 Arctic Skuas bathing in bay.

South Uist, Outer Hebrides   14.30

After a cool eight years, finally unblocked this one—the ♂ Steller's Eider located standing around on shoreline rocks with about 30 Eiders.

A comparatively small, angular duck and strikingly patterned despite the beginnings of moult into eclipse. Plumage basically black and white, with rich cinnamon-orange wash on under-parts, darkest on lower belly and very distinctive at any distance. On close approach seen to have white head with green lumps, black collar and breast spots and black and white patterned upper-parts. Large white patches showing on closed wing, and purply-blue speculum bordered by a white, down-curved band. Bill and legs appeared dark greyish. When swimming showed a surprisingly long, pointed tail, held cocked.

Several small groups of Twites feeding on rough ground, flying up with characteristic buzzing call-notes.

One female long-tailed Duck swimming around on pool behind beach. A stocky duck with small head and bill, and steep forehead.

Steller's Eider. There have been only 14 records of this vagrant from Arctic Russia and Siberia, but this individual has been present, off and on, since 1972.

Long-tailed Duck. A winter visitor in large numbers, but only occasionally summering.

Plumage rather nondescript brownish and white, with pale face and dark cheek patches.

Several Hooded Crows hanging around beach, causing some consternation to a small colony of Common Gulls.

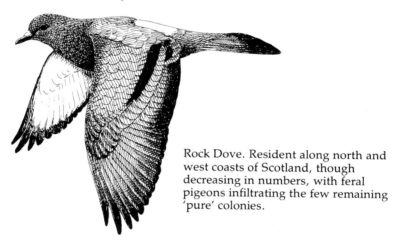

Rock Dove. Resident along north and west coasts of Scotland, though decreasing in numbers, with feral pigeons infiltrating the few remaining 'pure' colonies.

Benbecula   18.30
Several Eiders and Tufted Ducks with chicks around coast, and 10 Shovelers on a reed-fringed loch. Many Arctic Terns, Corn Buntings, Meadow Pipits and Wheatears beside road.

North Uist   19.00
One Rock Dove flying, showing the unique combination of pale grey upper-parts, contrasting with darker foreparts, white rump and under-wings, and short black wing-bars.

One or two Corncrakes heard calling intermittently during the evening from marshy meadows, the birds remaining hidden in sedges. One ♂ Hen Harrier flew across fields, gliding off around distant hillside.

Few other birds seen besides 1 light-phase Arctic Skua flying overhead, and a party of 3 Red-throated Divers flying over Lochmaddy, out to the harbour.

[93]

Ferry crossing, Lochmaddy to Uig   06.30–08.40

Greylag Goose. Mainly winter visitor, but wild birds breed in NW Scotland and Hebrides. Feral populations have been established in Norfolk, Kent and elsewhere.

Party of 10 Greylag Geese watched grazing on small island in bay. Typically large, grey geese with quite pale neck and head, large orange bill and pink legs.

Seabirds seen on the crossing similar to yesterday; 150+ Manx Shearwaters including a party of about 80 birds bathing in harbour. Many Gannets, thousands of Guillemots, Razorbills, Puffins and Kittiwakes (especially nearer Skye) and a few Black Guillemots seen.

Also about 25 separate Storm Petrels dashing around low over sea. Seen to be small petrels with square, or perhaps slightly rounded, tail, blackish-brown in colour with contrasting white rump and narrow white line on under-wings.

Also 4 Arctic Skuas flew south, and 1 Great Skua followed the boat for some while.

Storm Petrel. Mainly summer visitor, breeding in colonies from Scillies along west and northern coasts of Britain.

One Raven and a Buzzard sparring over hilltop on Skye, and several Hooded Crows along road.

[94]

Crested Tit. The resident British race is confined to Scotland, principally in the Spey valley.

Cairngorms

Poor views of one of the famous Ospreys at Loch Garten, crouched low down on nest in steady drizzle, with only the head visible.

One Crested Tit moving through the pines, located by distinctive call—a short, purring trill. Unmistakable little bird with erect crest and black and white face-markings. Several more heard calling later.

One female Capercaillie flew from undergrowth near track—the usual gross performance, being very big and very noisy. Seen to be a mottled brown bird, distinctly orangy on the breast, with a long, rounded tail.

Due to the dreadful weather—constant rain—and despite quite extensive searching, none of the other Cairngorm specialities (Scottish Crossbill, Black Grouse and Ptarmigan) could be located—another Osprey, hovering over the far side of the loch, but not diving, was the only other bird of note seen.

Capercaillie. This game-bird, having become extinct in the 18th century, is now well distributed over much of Scotland after being successfully re-introduced in the 19th century.

[95]

Sheringham, Norfolk 15.00–16.00
The adult Sabine's Gull seen again, feeding and resting on calm sea several hundred yards off sea-front. After a while it flew off west, apparently heading off inland.
    A party of 20 Common Scoter flew east.

Cley, Norfolk 17.30–19.45
Scattering of usual waders on reserve, including 3 Black-tailed Godwits and 5+ Ruff, but evidence of return wader passage with 1 Green Sandpiper, 3 Common Sandpipers, 3+ Spotted Redshanks, 2 Greenshanks and 1 Golden Plover seen in the evening. The summering male Scaup and 1 Pochard seen from Daukes' Hide, while breeding birds included several Shelducks with broods of highly animated black and white young and a family party of Bearded Tits, which included 7+ young.

Shelduck. Common in most suitable coastal areas.

Bearded Tit. Though prone to suffer in severe winters, seems to be well established in several areas, the stronghold being in East Anglia.

[96]

Cley, Norfolk   07.30–09.00

Similar birds again on reserve, the waders seen including 3 Whimbrels, 6 Dunlin, 3 Common Sandpipers, 10 Ruff and 1 Spotted Redshank, while the ♂ Scaup was still present. More unusual were 3 Eiders on the sea, and 1 Guillemot standing mournfully on shingle beach.

Scaup. Mainly a winter visitor, with odd birds only rarely summering, though it has bred in N Scotland.

Two juvenile Little Gulls swimming on small pool at the Quags. One recently-fledged Black Redstart perched on top of crabapple tree at Weybourne—a rather dingy, 'scaly' version of ♀.

Sheringham, Norfolk   13.20

A few Fulmars and Kittiwakes flying past, and 1 ♂ Kestrel flew west, out at sea.

At 14.20, the same adult Sabine's Gull flew in along the beach. Watched for an hour mostly around the promenade, swooping gracefully around just a few yards offshore, often fluttering over calmer water between the groynes with a few Black-headed Gulls (which apparently acted as a lure when fed with bread!). Also seen perched on groyne piles.

Smashing bird, though seemingly losing much of the hood. At close range, white inner webs of primaries noted while fluttering over beach, and showing chevron-patterned wing-tips at rest.

Sabine's Gull. The same individual as first seen on July 9—a delightful summer bonus.

The Brecks, Suffolk   11.30

Three Stone-curlews (located by chance, at a different site to June 14) watched on turf clearings on slope—wary birds usually slinking off behind various scattered gorse bushes, and one bird quite effectively concealing itself by standing 'frozen' in the dappled shadows of a dead bush.

Also 1 Red-backed Shrike hunting from nearby gorse.

Titchwell, Norfolk   15.00

Following reports of a 'Black Heron', arrived to find it was indeed just that—a melanistic Grey Heron, watched feeding in creeks and flying. An impressive bird, presumably a juvenile, appearing completely black at a glance, but in fact with dark grey mantle and wing-coverts, paler area from bill to eye and a little yellow showing on feet and lower mandible.

The adult Gull-billed Tern was still present, patrolling around the tern colony on the beach, occasionally landing on the gravel, just in front of the hide. Plumage perhaps now a little abraded, and showing more dark in the primaries.

On the freshwater scrape were 5 Little Gulls, 2 Ruff and about 5 Green Sandpipers. Eight Whimbrels flew over west, and 1 Wood Sandpiper heard calling.

Four Marsh Harriers were perched on dead trees in the reed-bed, with very upright 'shouldery' stance, three in dark all-over plumage showing creamy head-markings—presumably immatures.

One Common Scoter and 1 ♂ Velvet Scoter were seen on the sea, the latter being slightly larger, with a long-headed appearance, with white wing and face patches.

Melanistic Grey Heron.

[98]

Velvet Scoter. Mostly winter visitor, and passage migrant, a few birds occasionally summer.

Also seen here was 1♂ Red-backed Shrike, flying around the car park, perching on spindly saplings, a very confiding individual.

Cley, Norfolk   18.30

Apart from the ♂ Scaup, 1 Little Gull and 2 Wigeon, there was a fair scattering of migrant waders on the reserve, including about 30 Ruff, 5 Spotted Redshanks, 2 Greenshanks, several Common and Green Sandpipers and 1 Wood Sandpiper. Also 1 Whimbrel, 1 Black-tailed Godwit, 7 Golden Plovers and, more interestingly, 1 Little Ringed Plover and 16 Curlew Sandpipers were noted.

W3 ———————————— *July 27* ———————— **warm and sunny**

Cley, Norfolk   08.00

Much the same waders present as yesterday, including 7 Greenshanks, several Spotted Redshanks, 15 Curlew Sandpipers, 10 Dunlin and 1 Whimbrel, but also 1 Little Stint.

One Green, 1 Common and 1 Wood Sandpiper feeding side by side just in front of Bittern Hide provided a good opportunity to compare the three species, while 45 Avocets in the air together over the reserve, shrieking, was just splendid!

Three juvenile Wheatears by North Hide, presumably local birds.

Avocets. Away from the East Anglian colonies, a regular visitor in small numbers to southern coasts.

[99]

Adult Little Gull (with Black-headed Gulls).

Teesside, Cleveland   16.00

Perhaps not the most picturesque of birding areas, it gets its fair share of cripplers, though today's was a fruitless visit, there being no sign of the reported White-rumped Sandpiper, and the Long-tailed Skua failed to perform for us.

Among the birds seen were several Little Gulls, including a summer-plumaged adult roosting with Black-headeds, and a variety of the commoner waders.

Nine Curlew Sandpipers, 1 Wood and 5+ Green Sandpipers, 5 Greenshanks, 1 Spotted Redshank, several Whimbrels and 10+ Golden Plovers were noted on the marshy pools, as well as 250+ roosting Curlews. As the tide ebbed, hundreds of Dunlin and Knot appeared in the estuary, nearly all of the latter in the faded orange and grey summer plumage.

In the evening, 3 Arctic Skuas were patrolling the river-mouth, occasionally harrying passing terns.

Knot. Very large numbers winter in the major estuaries of the east and west coasts, also occurring as a passage migrant.

[100]

One Barn Owl flew across road, in headlights, near Barton Mills. One Buzzard perched on roadside telegraph pole near Camborne.

Porthgwarra, Cornwall   07.00

Cory's Shearwaters (20–24) moving past westwards, some birds circling back east, then off west. Most birds about 1 mile offshore, flying past the Runnel-stone buoy. Although bill and leg colour impossible to see at this distance, readily identifiable by generally ashy-brown upper-parts and off-white under-parts, with smoky grey 'hood' extending onto cheeks and sides of upper breast. Some birds showing darker tail and flight feathers, a few with indistinct pale upper-tail coverts. Silky white under-wings edged with grey-brown. Large shearwaters, rather broad-winged and heavy bodied, with leisurely flight manner, including long 'flat' glides low over sea, with wings mostly held swept back and slightly downcurved. Also 80+ Manx Shearwaters, mostly moving west, including 15+ Balearic types (dark brownish birds, variably smudged below).

One adult Mediterranean Gull flew east, just offshore of rocks. Immaculate summer-plumaged bird, showing pure white wing-tips, strikingly red bill and complete black hood with white 'eyelid' blobs.

Few other birds seen on sea-watch apart from several Fulmars and Gannets, 1 Greenshank, 2 Dunlin and 1 Sanderling flying east, and a few Swifts flying east out at sea.

Cory's Shearwater. Pelagic, breeding East Atlantic and Mediterranean. Great Atlantic wanderers, rarely seen from coastal vantage points. Formerly less than 2,000 had ever been recorded in the British Isles, but in this, exceptional, autumn, unprecedented numbers were seen, including nearly 11,000 off Cape Clear in just one day!

Pair of Ravens loitering around clifftops.

One juvenile Cuckoo on rocks on headland, constantly chiping and being fed by host Rock Pipits.

Mediterranean Gull.

Carnsew Basin, Hayle Estuary, Cornwall

Restless flock of 14 Common Sandpipers rushing around pool edge, calling excitedly. One Wood Sandpiper flew over.

One full summer-plumaged Great Northern Diver in middle of pool, busily roll-preening. Very close views of a superb bird, attractively marked with black-and-white-chequered mantle, finely spotted wings and flanks and striped along sides of breast. Black head and neck glossed bottle-green, with broad collar-markings and fine 'chin-strap' spots. Heavy, dark grey, bill and blood-red eyes.

Great Northern Diver. Breeds Iceland. Generally distributed winter visitor to all coasts, commoner in north. Occasionally summers and has bred.

White-rumped Sandpiper. Breeds Arctic America, winters South America. Vagrant to Britain, though occurring annually, mostly in autumn.

Cley, Norfolk   19.00–20.30

Influx of waders onto the reserve, including 60+ Ringed Plovers and 30+ Snipe visible from Daukes' Hide.

Also 10+ Common, 3+ Green and 6+ Wood Sandpipers, 5+ Spotted Redshanks, 2 Greenshanks and 1 juvenile Little Ringed Plover.

About 35 Curlew Sandpipers on the main scrape appeared to be all adults, in various stages of moult, but several in full chestnut-orange summer plumage and 1 very silvery winter bird.

The 2 White-rumped Sandpipers watched feeding on Pat's Pool and the new Whitwell Scrape. Apparently adults, smaller than Dunlin and very grey-looking at distance. Very long-winged with short black legs and quite short black bill. White belly, supercilium and chin, while crown, cheeks and breast heavily striated dark grey. Upper-parts very scaly—neat dark-centred, pale-edged, coverts and tertials, mantle more patchy with occasional contrasting dark centred feathers on scapulars, and a few remaining gingery-edged feathers.

One bird less heavily-marked than the other with much plainer grey-coloured mantle.

In flight, noticeably long-winged and short-bodied, showing indistinct white wing-bar, obvious curved white rump and all-dark tail.

During the heavy rainstorm all the waders abandoned feeding and adopted a curious, though obviously practical, bittern-like posture with bills held skyward.

[103]

Suffolk   08.00–11.30
Golden Orioles (5+) singing—a strangely unreal experience, standing in the English countryside surrounded by these exotic liquid, fluty calls. Both the brilliant yellow and black males and greenish females, both with red bill, surprisingly difficult to locate in the tree canopy; mostly seen in swooping flight along the woodland rides. One bird squawking—the 'angry-cat', Jay-like call—near entrance of wood.

Few other birds seen besides the usual Tree Sparrows, Whitethroats and Blackcaps near the edge of the wood.

Golden Oriole. Summer visitor to most of Europe, rare but annual here in spring, breeding in small numbers at recently established colonies.

Cley, Norfolk   16.00–19.30
Perhaps fewer waders than yesterday. Apart from the Avocets, there were about 15 Dunlin, 15+ Ruff, 1 Bar-tailed Godwit and 2+ Spotted Redshanks.

Twenty-eight Curlew Sandpipers were counted, whilst around the reserve were 20+ Common, 3+ Green and 10+ Wood Sandpipers. Also 1–2 Little Ringed Plovers and 5 Little Stints.

The 2 White-rumped Sandpipers were still present, feeding on mud just a few yards away, in front of Bittern Hide. After a while they flew off, together, calling several times—distinctive quiet, very thin (mouse-like) 'jeet'. One bird watched later feeding just in front of Teal Hide.

Few other birds on marsh except 2 immature Little Gulls and 2 Wigeon. A brief look at the sea produced 1 dark-phase Arctic Skua flying east offshore and a first-summer Little Gull overhead, along the beach, calling.

Also 1 scaly-brown juvenile Cuckoo perched on reedstems just behind beach.

SE4 _____ *August 3* _____ sunny and warm

Cley, Norfolk   17.00–18.20

A count of the waders visible from Teal Hide in the evening produced 20+ Curlew Sandpipers, 6 Little Stints, 10 Dunlin, 15+ Common Sandpipers, 1 Green and 1 Wood Sandpiper, 5+ Spotted Redshanks and 1 Greenshank. Also 25+ Golden Plovers, 1 Whimbrel, 2 Bar-tailed Godwits and 10+ Ruff noted. The Avocet numbers were lower, 20+ birds being seen, as well as 2 Black-tailed Godwits, 20+ Snipe and 10+ Ringed Plovers. The 2 White-rumped Sandpipers were still present, spending much of the evening feeding just in front of the hide.

Among the duck were a few Gadwall and Shoveler and 20+ Teal.

Curlew Sandpiper and Dunlin, both in summer plumage. The former is basically a tundra-breeding east-coast passage migrant, occurring in fluctuating numbers. The latter is a common winter visitor, and a regular breeder in small numbers, mostly on the Scottish islands.

Short-eared Owl. Breeds sparingly in
north and west Britain, a winter visitor
elsewhere.

M9   06.10
One Short-eared Owl flew across dual-carriageway, landing on top-most sprig of a small pine tree, in the central reservation.

Aberuthven, Perth   06.40–07.40
The Black Stork located immediately, standing in a marshy field beside the River Earn, with 2 Herons. Flew to overgrown ox-bow, close to main road, where it stood about on bank of newly-dug mud beside drainage ditch for about ¾ hour. Disappeared into the ditch briefly before flying up and around the valley then back, to land for a short while on mud area, again with two Herons.

Presumably a second year bird, the upper-parts being blackish-brown, very smooth and slightly shiny but lacking the metallic sheen of full adult. Head dark brown, spongey mass of neck feathers slightly paler, though breast nearly as dark as mantle but showing some pale edgings. Under-parts, including 'thighs', creamy white. Heavy, reddish-brown, bill brighter and paler red towards tip, reddish legs and feet, and reddish cere and eye-patch noted, the irides being brown. Wings and tail completely blackish, the dark under-wing contrasting in flight with the white under-parts and 'armpits'.

After circling the valley for some time (not finding any thermal lift and having to flap strongly), the bird headed off along the distant northern ridge, and disappeared.

This is how twitching should be—the bird safely 'U.T.B.' before breakfast!

Black Stork. An extremely rare vagrant. Only 45 have ever been recorded in Britain, though has been seen annually in the last few years, possibly due to an apparent expansion of its European breeding range.

August 10

Prawle Point, Devon   05.30–13.30

About 50 Swallows hawking around car park soon after dawn. A thorough flogging of the area produced 25+ Whitethroats, 5 Blackcaps and 10+ Willow Warbler/Chiffchaffs, 10+ Stonechats and 3 Wheatears, but nothing resembling the reported Rufous Bush-chat.

One ♀/juvenile Redstart seen in the gardens in Prawle village.

Other birds included 1 Buzzard and 2 Ravens soaring around the headland, and 1 ♀ Sparrowhawk sparring with a party of 8 enraged Magpies in Pig-nose Valley.

One Melodious Warbler watched in sunny hedgerow, flying out (and occasionally hovering, flycatcher-style) over cornfield to catch insects. Typical *Hippolais*, rather bulky with long bill, plumage olivy-grey above and off-white/yellowish below, and a rather 'open-faced' expression (even though showing quite strong eye-stripe and supercilium). Legs and feet blue-grey in colour. Characteristic rounded head, large liquid eye, and shortish wings, showing no pale panel, noted.

A second bird, seen rather briefly in the coastguard's gardens, showed a greyer plumage and a strong pale wing panel.

Melodious Warbler. Breeds in SW Europe. Regular vagrant in small numbers, mostly on the south coast.

Porthgwarra, Cornwall   06.00–14.00

A protracted sea-watch resulted in 5+ Cory's Shearwaters, flying west at distance of the Runnel-stone buoy, with typical lazy action and rather nondescript plumage. 360+ Manx Shearwaters flew past west, in parties of up to 15 birds, with some also flying east or feeding far offshore. Two Balearic type Manx Shearwaters also flew past close by, separately; very dark individuals, sooty-brown all over with paler belly and wing-linings.

Sooty Shearwaters (3+) flew past separately, looking large but narrow-winged and showing completely dark plumage with pale wing-linings.

100+ Gannets appeared to be moving past west, with about 50 birds feeding offshore, plunging around fishing boats.

Other birds seen included 5 Arctic Skuas flying past west, and 3 Great Skuas, two of which stopped to harry the feeding Gannets and gulls.

Also about 25 Fulmars, about 15 Kittiwakes, 2 Common Scoter and 1 Puffin flew west.

Besides 2+ Whimbrels overhead and 1 Common Sandpiper heard, the only other birds noted on the headland were 2 Ravens, 1 Wheatear, 1 Stonechat, 3 Willow Warblers and 2 Whitethroats.

E2–4 _____ *August 16* _____ clear and sunny

Blakeney Point, Norfolk   15.15–19.15

A stroll up to the point and back revealed a few migrants: 18 Willow Warblers, 2+ Garden Warblers, 1 Whitethroat and 1 Sedge Warbler were seen in the sueda belt, also 1 Wheatear, 1 Whinchat, and 1 ♀ Pied Flycatcher in the tamarisks near the point.

One Spotted Redshank and 1 Green Sandpiper were feeding beside the pools in the dunes, while several Greenshanks, Whimbrels and 30+ Curlews were in Blakeney Harbour. Three Arctic Skuas flew overhead at the point.

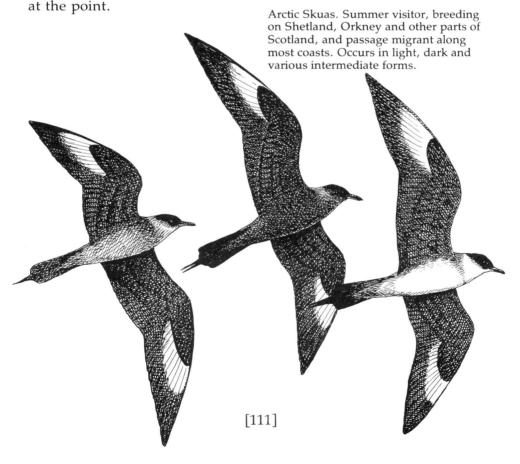

Arctic Skuas. Summer visitor, breeding on Shetland, Orkney and other parts of Scotland, and passage migrant along most coasts. Occurs in light, dark and various intermediate forms.

Cley, Norfolk   08.30

Waders on the reserve, seen from Daukes' and North Hide, included 25 Ruff, 6 Golden Plovers, 1 Whimbrel, 4 Dunlin, 1 Little Stint and 2 Greenshanks, 1 Common and 1 Green Sandpiper. Also 1 juvenile Little Ringed Plover, 6+ Spotted Redshanks (including one juvenile with dusky barred under-parts) and only 6 Avocets—the majority of summering adults having now moved off. Along at the Iron Road, 10 Dunlin, 2 Wood Sandpipers and 1 Curlew Sandpiper were feeding on the flooded fields, and also here was 1 Purple Sandpiper and a single White-rumped Sandpiper (looking distinctively long-winged and 'frosty' plumaged).

Few migrants were in the area besides Turtle Doves, Wheatears and 1 Spotted Flycatcher, while 2 immature Red-backed Shrikes further along the coast showed very scaly plumage and shortish tails, indicating they may have just recently fledged from nearby.

Very little seen at Holkham, and no sign of the Ruddy Shelduck at Livermere Lake. One Kingfisher, fishing from reedmace stems at the latter site provided a dazzling bonus, and 1 Spotted Redshank here, a species not too commonly seen inland.

Kingfisher. Resident on suitable stretches of water throughout England and Wales, moving to the coasts in severe winters.

[112]

Cley, Norfolk   15.00

A fairly short sea-watch was rewarded with a steady passage of sea-birds, all moving west, towards the Wash—a phenomenon which often occurs at Cley, presumably much to the chagrin of the birds when they run out of sea!

The majority were Kittiwakes, Commic and Sandwich Terns, but also an early, summer-plumaged, Red-throated Diver, 3+ Gannets, single Black Tern, Common Scoter, and Great Skua, and 20+ Arctic Skuas.

Several Curlews and Whimbrels, 3 Golden and 3 Grey Plovers also flew past offshore.

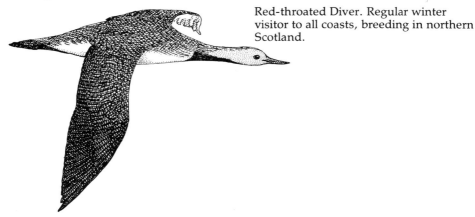

Red-throated Diver. Regular winter visitor to all coasts, breeding in northern Scotland.

On the reserve were 2 Bar-tailed Godwits, 2 Spotted Redshanks, 6+ Ruff, 10 Dunlin, 2 Common, 2 Wood and 2 Curlew Sandpipers, while at Weybourne Camp the only migrants appeared to be 1 Cuckoo, 1 Yellow Wagtail and 10 Turtle Doves. George, the local Glaucous Gull, was standing, preening, with roosting Black-headeds at the Quags. 1 adult Little Gull seen on the pools and one dark-mantled Herring Gull, possibly of one of the northern races, completed this assorted group.

Glaucous Gull. Though a regular winter visitor in small numbers, this individual has now returned to this area for 13 winters.

[113]

Oxwich, West Glam.   06.00–09.00

One Greenshank and 1 Wood Sandpiper heard calling over the marsh. One Green Woodpecker watched in beech trees on hillside—a juvenile, with face and under-parts heavily barred dark brown, and scaly pattern on upper-parts.

Pair of Ravens flew over, croaking, one bird 'rolling' several times—and 1 very neatly marked Buzzard perched in close trees. Five or more Herons flying over marsh and perched in treetops. The adult Purple Heron was eventually located standing quietly at the edge of close pool in reed-bed. 'Scoped for some time, mostly in a rather hunched pose, but often stretching up and peering around, and once flew a few yards.

Excellent bird, apparently a full adult with strong black stripes on 'snaky' rusty neck, very dark slaty-brown upper-parts with a distinctly purple patch on 'shoulders'. Large feet noticeable in flight, and yellow bill, eye, and upper part of leg also noted.

Purple Heron. Breeding widely in Europe, it is a rare, though annual, vagrant to Britain in summer.

Portland, Dorset

Having 'got' the heron, a visit to Portland on spec. proved rather fruitless, the only migrants seen being 5+ Willow Warblers and 2 Tree Pipits. 1 ♀ Sparrowhawk flew over Weston, mobbed by about 100 Linnets. At Radipole in the evening, 2 adult Little Gulls were seen with about 500 Black-headed Gulls, and 5 Greenshanks, 1 Dunlin, 1 Ruff and several Redshanks were feeding on the exposed mud. Other birds included 1 singing Cetti's Warbler, and large parties of roosting Swallows and Yellow Wagtails, twice panicked by a marauding juvenile Sparrowhawk.

ESE4 _____*August 25*_____ warm and sunny

Weymouth, Dorset

The morning, from dawn, was spent at Lodmoor, where the hoped-for Aquatic Warbler did not blunder into the ringer's net. Besides a singing Cetti's Warbler, 1 Greenshank, 1 Spotted Redshank, 1 Wood Sandpiper and 2 Ruff were perhaps noteworthy, and 1 Whinchat was seen perched on various bramble bushes.

One Garden Warbler and 1 leucistic House Sparrow were the highlights of Portland Bill.

Staines Reservoir, Surrey 15.00

Several Great Crested Grebes and many Tufted Duck and Pochard scattered on the southern half of the reservoir.

On the northern side, 4 Black-necked Grebes were swimming some distance from the causeway. One bird was an adult, still in virtually complete summer plumage, the golden cheek-fan and reddish flanks contrasting with blackish upper-parts and black head and neck. The other three appeared to be juveniles, with smudgey grey-brown plumage, buffish on neck.

Black-necked Grebe. Though breeding in very small numbers, mainly a passage migrant and winter visitor, to both coastal and inland waters.

Drift Reservoir, Cornwall   06.15–08.00

At least six Common and 3+ Green Sandpipers feeding in muddy bays, also 1 Oystercatcher, 3 Greenshanks, 2 Dunlin and 1 very tame Curlew Sandpiper seen along edge of reservoir.

One Lesser Yellowlegs located on grassy shoreline. 'Scoped at about 40 yards and seen to resemble a slim, elegant Redshank, but rather smaller, with very long, slender legs and straight fine bill. Plumage basically dark grey above, liberally speckled with white and with some darker feather-centres, striated grey on head, neck and breast, with pale supercilium and eye-ring, white below. Bill and eye black, legs yellow (though perhaps not as bright as some), the latter extending beyond the tail in flight, when square white rump, finely barred tail and unmarked wings also noticeable.

Called several times—'hu hu hu', rather similar to Greenshank but lacking the strength or ringing quality, and occasionally only as a double note.

Lesser Yellowlegs. North America.
Virtually an annual vagrant, over 140
have been recorded in Britain, nearly all
in autumn.

Buzzard. One of the few relatively successful raptors in Britain, locally common in the south west, Wales and Scotland.

Marazion Marsh, Cornwall   08.15–09.45

The Aquatic Warbler reported from the previous day failed to appear, only Reed and Sedge Warblers seen along the edge of the reed-bed, some of the latter being juveniles showing distinct central crown stripes.

One Peregrine Falcon flew across marsh, coming low in front of pines to show head pattern, bluey upper-parts, etc., flushing 24 Herons which circled together over the copse. Also here were 4 Buzzards, soaring overhead, calling, and 1 Little Gull flying around over the sea offshore.

Sedge Warbler, a rather common summer visitor to most of the British Isles.

Drift Reservoir (NE Corner), Cornwall   10.30–19.15

Similar birds seen again, including the Lesser Yellowlegs, but also several Ravens, 1 Buzzard and 10+ Yellow Wagtails.

After a further 8 hours wait, the Solitary Sandpiper silently materialised, feeding in the muddy corner of the reservoir. A rather small, neat, Green Sandpiper-type bird, larger than the accompanying Common Sandpipers (with proportionately slightly longer bill).

Upper-parts brownish spotted with off-white, more so towards rear, where the white spots on edges of tertials forming a barred effect. Under-parts white with smudgey grey-brown breast patches, head quite dark with pale chin, oval white spot above dark stripe between eye and bill (and pale patch below) and characteristic neat, unbroken, white 'spectacles'.

Cocked tail downwards several times to show blackish rump and centre of tail, latter with white, black-barred outer feathers (this pattern extending onto the upper-tail coverts).

Flew around bay on flicked, bowed wings, with head held high. Clean-cut tail pattern and lack of white rump giving a rather long-ended impression, and dusky-grey under-wings noted (not as dark as Green Sandpiper). Call in flight 'peet weet weet', similar to Green Sandpiper but lacking the urgent, ringing quality.

Solitary Sandpiper. North America.
Only the 20th ever recorded in Britain.
All have been in autumn.

[118]

September 1

Levington Pools, R. Orwell, Suffolk   18.45–20.15

With no sign of the Wilsons' Phalarope, a fruitless visit, the only birds noted being the commoner waders roosting on dredged-mud pans, 1 Sedge Warbler flushed from the sea wall, and 1 Tawny Owl seen at dusk, perched on roadside telegraph pole.

Tawny Owl. A common resident.

September 2

Levington Pools, Suffolk   18.45–20.15

Another evening visit drew a blank, 2 Greenshanks and 5 Tufted Ducks on the mud pans providing little compensation.

September 3

Weybourne Camp, Norfolk   05.45–08.00

Parties of Swallows moving over soon after dawn.

Parties, also, of juvenile Mistle Thrushes.

One ♀ Sparrowhawk hunting along hillside, flicking over hedge and through field full of Linnets and Goldfinches. With neither sight nor sound of the Sardinian Warbler located yesterday, a thorough search of the area did produce a few migrants—Wheatear, Garden Warbler and 4+ Whinchats in the bushes, and 2+ Wrynecks, the latter seen on various parts of the camp and apparently moving around together. One bird rather neatly marked was seen sunbathing with all feathers fluffed-up, assuming a 'spiky hedgehog' pose.

Other migrants: 1 Grey Wagtail over, and 2 Ruff flying eastwards.

Levington Pools, Suffolk   10.00–11.30, 14.00–19.30

Again no Wilson's Phalarope—or anything else, come to that.

[119]

Landguard Point, Felixstowe, Suffolk   12.00–13.30
Several migrants in the bushes around the fort, including Garden Warbler, Lesser Whitethroat, 1 Whinchat and 2 Pied Flycatchers.

The juvenile Barred Warbler was located after a little time, feeding in brambles overhanging the moat, and later in elderberry bushes. A very heavy, long-looking warbler, pale overall with buffy-grey upper-parts merging into creamy under-parts. Distinctive off-white double wing-bars noted, as well as pale grey-buff edgings to tertials and secondaries, and minimal barring on vent area. Rather featureless expression with dark eye, diffuse dark eye-stripe with paler line above. Heavy bill pale horn-coloured, edged darker, legs and feet dull greyish. An amazingly clumsy bird, blundering around in the bushes, and flying with shrike-like action; with large wings and long, slightly rounded, tail.

Also 1 Wryneck watched feeding on sunny bank on dunes, under tamarisk bushes.

Barred Warbler. A regular autumn visitor in very small numbers, mostly to the north and east coasts, virtually all being immature birds.

=============================*September 4*=============================

Weybourne Camp, Norfolk   17.45–19.45
One or two Wrynecks watched around the mound, returning at dusk to roost in the apple tree.

SW4 ————————————————*September 5*———— cloudy with showers

Weybourne Camp, Norfolk   13.15–19.35
Few migrants seen besides 2 Lesser Whitethroats and 2+ Whinchats. After rapidly losing faith in the presence of the Sardinian Warbler, it was heard to call twice from the dense blackthorn hedge—a distinctive, loud, staccato rattle.

Whinchat. Summer visitor, breeding in much of northern Britain and Wales, and elsewhere a common passage migrant, especially in autumn.

Weybourne Camp, Norfolk   06.15–19.30

Though heard to call once, the Sardinian Warbler again refused to be seen. A few migrants in evidence including 10+ Whitethroats, 3 Lesser Whitethroats, 1 Blackcap, several Chiffchaffs and Turtle Doves, while 1 Red-backed Shrike and 1 Wryneck were more unusual.

Among the local residents were Corn Bunting and a party of 8 Bullfinches (including 1 ♂ in adult plumage but with an unmarked buffy head).

Corn Bunting. Patchily distributed over much of Britain, its disappearance from many areas may be connected with modern farming techniques and the loss of hedgerow habitat.

[121]

Chigborough Farm Gravel Pits, Maldon, Essex 07.30–08.15
One Greenshank heard calling before dawn, only Redshank, Snipe and Ringed Plover on the pits first thing.

At 07.50, the Wilson's Phalarope flew in and began feeding actively along the water's edge, around mud islands, giving excellent views in the morning sunshine.

A typical winter/juvenile bird, sleek-looking but rather pot-bellied with long thin neck and small head. Plumage very pale overall with white under-parts, smoked grey on neck and sides of upper breast, and a very pale grey wash on flanks. Crown and ear-patch darker, contrasting with white face, forehead and supercilium, latter fading down onto side of neck. Upper-parts grey, virtually unmarked on mantle, with browner, pale-edged wing coverts and darker brown tertials with prominent creamy edges. Rather shortish dull yellow legs, fine, straight black bill and dark eye noted.

Wilson's Phalarope. North America. Since the first record in 1954, has become increasingly more regular in Britain, and is now recorded annually, mostly in autumn.

Comparatively stocky-looking in flight, with retracted neck, and feet barely projecting beyond tail. Wings virtually unmarked, dark above and pale below, square white rump and rounded tail white with fine grey barring.

Ring Ouzel. Regular passage migrant and summer visitor with some continental birds joining the east coast passage.

Landguard Point, Felixstowe, Suffolk   09.00–10.45

One immature Red-backed Shrike perched on brambles and flying around fortress moat—a very gingery, heavily scalloped individual.

One Ring Ouzel watched on elderberry bushes, a very dark bird with highly contrasting pale scaling on plumage and light grey wings. Calling—a hard 'tak tak'.

Red-backed Shrike. More often seen now as a passage migrant than as a breeding bird.

Easthaugh Gravel Pits, Lyng, Norfolk   11.15

One Pectoral Sandpiper located easily and 'scoped feeding along near edge of small grassy island in pit. A very neat wader, as is usual with this species, though this individual appeared quite bulky. Dark upper-parts with all feathers edged paler, showing two distinct pale lines on mantle, a rather rusty cap and off-white supercilium tapering behind eye. Under-parts white (with, on this bird, a rather dirty grey-buff wash), the heavily streaked breast region ending abruptly above the belly (though extending slightly as a dark smudge on the upper flanks). Shortish, slightly decurved bill dark, legs and feet dull ochre in colour.

Pectoral Sandpiper. Breeds in NE Siberia and Arctic North America, wintering in South America, annually occurring in Britain, most often in the autumn.

The rest of the day was spent at Weybourne Camp—yet again, the elusive Sardinian Warbler failed to materialise.

W4 _____ *September 9* _____ mainly sunny

Blithfield Reservoir, Staffs   07.00–07.45

The Buff-breasted Sandpiper located feeding along turf and gravel spit across corner of reservoir, looking about size of Ringed Plover but with small rounded head and peculiar crouchy pigeon-like feeding gait.

[124]

Plumage a clean pinkish honey-buff all over with near blackish speckling on crown and sides of upper breast, and mottled upper-parts with a neat scaly appearance due to pale feather edgings. Beady black eye, with a pale buff surround, short blackish bill (perhaps very slightly decurved) and dull chrome-orange legs and feet noted.

Generally holding a rather hunched pose, but occasionally stretching up to show longish neck, then, with longish wings, appearing quite streamlined.

Also 3 Dunlin, 2 Little Stints and 1 Ruff were feeding nearby, and 1 Sparrowhawk flew across the reservoir, low over the water.

Dunlin and Little Stints.

Buff-breasted Sandpiper. Arctic North America, wintering South America. Formerly much rarer, now an annual, mostly autumn, visitor.

[125]

North Norfolk   14.00–19.30

Very little at Holme besides a group of 100 Sanderling gathered around pool on sandflats, while hundreds of Coot and various ducks were scattered over the freshwater pool at Titchwell, including 25+ Wigeon.

Groups of waders feeding on the floating vegetation here included 1 Greenshank, 2+ Ruff, 8+ Curlew Sandpipers and 12+ Little Stints. Along at Cley, 1 Curlew Sandpiper and 1 Little Stint were feeding at the Eye pool, 1 Greenshank, 1 Spotted Redshank, 1 Green Sandpiper and only 3 Avocets were among the few waders visible from Daukes' Hide.

A single Little Ringed Plover and 1 Wood Sandpiper flew over the reserve, calling.

Finally, another visit to Weybourne Camp proved fruitless.

Little Stint. Regular passage migrant, chiefly in autumn to coastal areas. Breeds in northern Russia.

September 11

On a before-work visit to Draycote Water, Warwickshire, the Spotted Sandpiper could not be located in the short time available

September 12

Staines Reservoir, Surrey   18.45

Many ducks, Coots, etc., all sheltering close in to the bank in a severe gale but 180+ Great Crested Grebes forming a loose raft, far out in the choppy water. Nine or more winter-plumaged Black-necked Grebes in the near corner of reservoir, some diving but most hunched-up against the wind. Very dusky birds, the sleeping birds showing just a little white on breast and belly.

Black-necked Grebe. The London reservoirs are traditionally a favourite for this species.

Draycote Water, Warks 16.00

One Common Sandpiper in bay.

The juvenile Spotted Sandpiper watched feeding along edge of reservoir, quickly moving along gravel sections, pausing longer to pick insects off rolls of storm-blown weed. Though similar to Common Sandpiper, generally cleaner plumage, perhaps dumpier-looking (due to noticeably shorter tail) and slightly longer-legged.

Pale grey-brown upper-parts with plain-coloured tertials lacking the patterned fringes of Common Sandpiper, and strong barring on wing-coverts. Under-parts clean white with brownish chest-smudges. Also showing a neat pale eye-ring, paleish brown bill with darker tip, and bright yellow legs and feet.

Spotted Sandpiper. North America. A rare vagrant to Britain with 50 records, mostly in the autumn. Virtually annual in recent years, the identification criteria have only recently been fully established.

Frodsham Pools, Cheshire   19.00

The Spotted Crake soon appeared, skulking around the base of the reedmace, often out in the open but always moving with typical apprehensive action, head held low and tail cocked, with flexed legs. Upper-parts olive-brown with dark centred, buff-edged feathers streaked with white. Crown and cheeks mottled brownish, rest of head and under-parts blue-grey, liberally spotted with white and barred on flanks. Characteristic rich buff under-tail coverts most obvious. Small-ish yellowish bill with red base, legs and large feet green in colour. Incredibly small-looking compared with the nearby Moorhens.

Spotted Crake. Mostly a scarce autumn passage migrant though with its elusive character may well be largely overlooked.

SW6 ───────────*September 14*─────────── mostly sunny

New Brighton, Merseyside   07.00–09.00

At least two of the hoped-for 'left-over' Leach's Petrels were still present in the river-mouth area, flying into the wind and working across bay.

One of these birds came very close inshore, feeding by hanging on the wind with angled wings, low over the water, and occasionally pattering on the surface. Fairly large petrels with long pointed wings, and 'lumpy' forked tail visible at some distance. Plumage blackish overall with 'wrapped around' white rump showing greyer central line at very close range, greyer forewing and broad pale diagonal bar on upper-wing.

One seen flying over sandbar later with determined but erratic, flight action.

Leach's Petrel. In Britain breeds on remote north-western islands, normally very rarely seen on inshore waters, most often only as a result of severe gales.

A few other birds seen in the river-mouth, including 8+ Little Gulls and 5+ Manx Shearwaters (2 of which were seen well into the river), and several Kittiwakes. One adult Sabine's Gull flew out of the river, past lighthouse, exhibiting the hyper-distinctive black, white and grey wing pattern and forked tail. Landed in distance on sandbar.

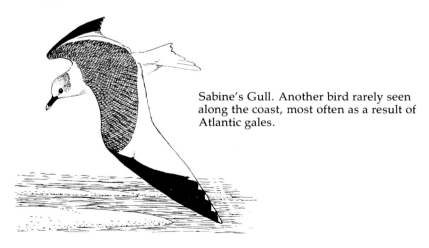

Sabine's Gull. Another bird rarely seen along the coast, most often as a result of Atlantic gales.

[129]

Blithfield Reservoir, Staffs   11.30

The Buff-breasted Sandpiper seen again, on far muddy shore, feeding, bathing and flying (when white under-wings contrasting with brown upper-wings noted). Among other birds here were 20+ Snipe, 1 Spotted Redshank, 5 Ruff and 1 yellow-legged Common Sandpiper. A group of 30 Cormorants perched on nearby treestumps looked rather out of place so far inland.

SW4 _____*September 16*___ foggy early, sunny later

One Barn Owl flew across the road at Bodmin, in car head-lights.

Stithians Reservoir, Cornwall   07.00–11.00, 16.40–17.35

The Semi-palmated Sandpiper watched from the Golden Lion causeway—grilled down to about 20 feet, feeding unconcernedly along muddy shoreline.

Basically similar to Little Stint though appearing a little larger, squarer-headed and stouter-bodied. Overall, rather pale-looking with 'frosty' buff and grey patterned upper-parts: finely striated mantle with whitish 'braces', double band of dark-centred, gingery-edged scapulars, and outer scapulars (and some median coverts?) with distinct 'anchor-marks' formed by dark centre and subterminal bar to otherwise pale feathers. Tertials and wing coverts grey-brown, edged broadly with pale buff. Head quite pale with finely streaked nape, quite strong brownish mask and streaked brown cap. Under-parts white with a buffish-grey suffusion on upper chest with a semi-gorget of fine dark striations. Black bill fairly long-looking, stouter at the base and definitely 'blob-ended' (this visible only at close range, and then only when viewed head-on). Blackish legs and feet, the semi-webbing between the toes occasionally discernible, at only very close range.

Semi-palmated Sandpiper. Only the 7th British record of this tricky peep which is the commonest of its group on the coasts of Eastern America.

The bird gave several different calls, including a rapid string of 'tet' notes, basically Little Stintish but of a 'woollier' quality, and a more distinctive 'tut ... tut ... cherk' or 'chut ... chut .... churrt'.

Other birds seen on the two visits included 1 Pectoral Sandpiper at the southern causeway, which while basically resembling the Lyng bird, looked smaller with more contrasting rufousy upper-parts, whiter below, with distinctly orangy legs.

Also 1 Spotted Redshank, and 3 Common Scoters (apparently of the American race).

Aquatic Warbler. Primarily a rare autumn passage vagrant, with a proportion of the records being birds trapped at south-coast reed-bed ringing stations.

Marazion Marsh, Cornwall   15.50–16.15

Dipped-in on 1 Aquatic Warbler, watched at the edge of phragmites bed, having just flown from area of short juncus.

A very pale, yellowish-looking bird with distinctive head pattern—yellow-buff face, broad supercilia, double black crown stripes bordering a clear, virtually white, central stripe. Yellowy-grey/buff upper-parts blotched blackish and gorget of fine streaks (extending onto flanks) suggesting the bird was probably an adult. Very broad pale edges to tertials, streaked rump and spiky tail also noted. Legs and bill pale creamy coloured, latter with dark tip.

Also, 1 Cetti's Warbler heard singing from reed-bed.

An hour's sea-watch from Porthgwarra in mid-afternoon produced a few Gannets and Kittiwakes, 3 Sandwich Terns, 6+ Arctic Skuas, 2 Great Skuas, 1 Little Gull and 1 Sooty Shearwater, all moving west.

September 18 hot and sunny

Mepal, Cambs   12.30–16.30
On the strength of a rumoured Roller, the afternoon was spent searching a wide area around the River Ouse, but with no result. 80+ Golden Plovers, 20+ Snipe, 1 Greenshank and 1 Lesser Whitethroat were the only birds noted.

September 20 dense fog

Bamburgh, Northumberland   18.30–19.30
After flogging the golf-course in minimal visibility the only birds remotely resembling the reported Isabelline Wheatear were 2 Greenland Wheatears—Meadow Pipit and Pied Wagtail being the other highlights of the visit.

September 21

With dense fog still blanketing Bamburgh, the episode was put down to experience and we headed south, arriving at Weybourne Camp (where it was clear, warm and sunny) to be gripped off by accounts of the Sardinian Warbler having been seen earlier.

Weybourne Camp, Norfolk
One juvenile Barred Warbler was seen here, leaping around between various bushes by the radar station, with typical strong flight action and showing grey-buff plumage with distinctive double wing-bars, and looking perhaps rather thrush-like at times.

Immature Barred Warbler, the second of three seen this autumn.

Other migrants here included 3+ Whinchats, 1 Redstart, several Wheatears and 2+ Lesser Whitethroats, while a brief look from Daukes' Hide at Cley revealed 50+ Ruff, 5+ Avocets, 2+ Curlew Sandpipers, 1 Spotted Redshank and 1 Greenshank.

September 23

Weybourne Camp, Norfolk 07.15–10.30

Several Whitethroats and Lesser Whitethroats seen, and a distinct influx of Song Thrushes noted.

The elusive Sardinian Warbler heard calling and subsinging during the morning, and eventually located in the copse at the top of the camp. The bird was watched from inside the copse moving through the foliage within the canopy, subsinging, and seen to be a stunning adult ♂.

Rather slender *Sylvia* with rounded tail and peaked crown; plumage sooty-grey above with blackish wings (with pale feather edgings) and blackish tail (with white outer feathers), and the under-parts paler smoky-grey. The clear cut, silky-white throat contrasted sharply with the black hood, as did the bird's most conspicuous feature at such close range—the red eye surrounded by bright red swollen orbital ring. Pale-based bill and legs brownish in colour.

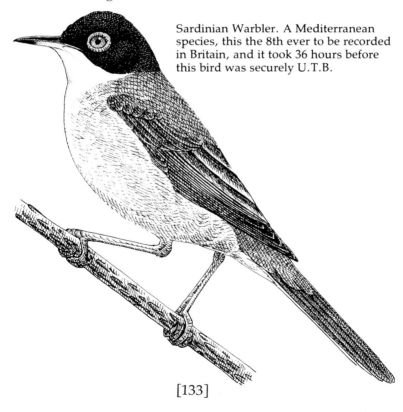

Sardinian Warbler. A Mediterranean species, this the 8th ever to be recorded in Britain, and it took 36 hours before this bird was securely U.T.B.

[133]

Brambling. A regular winter visitor in fluctuating numbers from Scandinavia.

Holkham (Wells end), Norfolk   12.15–15.00

Few migrants besides 1 Wheatear, 1 Blackcap, 1 Pied Flycatcher, a few Chiffchaffs, and 2 Swifts.

One ♂ Brambling with a party of Redpolls, retaining much of its summer plumage and quite strikingly black-and-orange-coloured, with white rump.

A small group of Egyptian Geese grazing in fields beside the road—peculiarly unattractive birds.

Cley, Norfolk   16.15–18.00

Among the birds seen from North Hide and Daukes' were large numbers of the wintering duck—250+ Wigeon, 200+ Teal and quite a few Shovelers and Pintail noted, also a flock of 86 feral Greylag Geese. About 100 Golden Plovers were present, as well as 60+ Ruff, 10+ Bar-tailed Godwits, 5+ Black-tailed Godwits, 6+ Avocets, 3 Greenshanks and 1 Spotted Redshank.

Apart from the ducks and waders, migrants were limited to 250+ Swallows over the reserve, 1 Wheatear, 3+ Swifts, and 1 Reed Warbler (in ivy at Walsey Hills).

Egyptian Goose. One of the recent additions to the British list, an introduced species with a flourishing free-flying colony at Holkham.

[134]

Jack Snipe. Widely distributed winter
visitor, but usually in very small
numbers at any one site.

Nene Valley, Northants   06.45–07.30

One Ruff, 1 Dunlin and 60+ Snipe seen at one of the pits and 1 Jack
Snipe flew up, silently and without zig-zagging, and circled past showing pointed all-dark tail, shortish bill and characteristic head pattern.

One Hobby flew across the pits, then low and fast over rooftops of the
town. Smashing little falcon, a real shifter despite apparently effortless
wing-action, with wings held swept-back. Distinctive shape with long
wings and narrow tail (usually showing slightly longer central feathers),
bluey upper-parts and characteristic black and white face-pattern
noted.

One ♂ Kestrel seen over slope, sparring with a Carrion Crow.

Hobby. Summer visitor, breeding in
small numbers in the southern counties
and rarely elsewhere in England.

[135]

Holkham (W. wood), Norfolk   14.30–16.30

Apparently a small movement of Lapwings flying west and an influx of Song Thrushes into the wood.

A party of Fieldfares flew over, calling, and other migrants included 5+ Blackcaps, 1 Spotted Flycatcher, 1 Redstart and 1 late Swift.

Cley, Norfolk   17.30

Winter waterfowl building up numbers, with 750+ Wigeon now on the reserve, and fewer waders in evidence—a few Golden Plover, 40+ Ruff and 20+ Snipe seen from hide, and only 2+ Avocets, 1 Spotted Redshank and 2 Curlew Sandpipers.

One particularly fine ♂ Bearded Tit watched in reeds beside track, exhibiting a touch of the oriental with its blue-grey, pink and orange plumage, highlighted with patches of black and white.

23.20. On return from the pub to the 'beach hotel', a smashing Barn Owl seen perched on roadside telegraph poles in the car head-lights, performing for some time before silently disappearing.

Barn Owl. A widespread resident in the British Isles, but nowhere numerous.

Holkham (Wells end), Norfolk   07.00–9.30
One Tawny Owl perched on gutter in car park during the night.

Siskin. Mainly a winter visitor in fluctuating numbers from Scandinavia, though it does breed in Scotland and some areas of England.

Very few birds seen in the wood, 2+ Redwings and 2 Siskins representing the winter birds, and several Blackcaps and 8 Chiffchaffs the only summer migrants.

Cley, Norfolk   11.45
A short sea-watch from the coastguards produced 80 Brent Geese, 20 Wigeon and 1 Red-throated Diver flying west, 1 Gannet, 20 Common Scoter and 5 Sandwich Terns flying east.

One ♀ Scaup swimming on the Eye Pool—appeared happy to remain on this puddle, allowing very close approach.

One rather handsome Hooded Crow strolling around in meadow beside the Iron road.

Weybourne Camp, Norfolk   12.15–14.15
Two Blackcaps and 1 Chiffchaff were the only summer migrants seen, and 1 Lapland Bunting flew west overhead, calling.

Hooded Crow. Breeds commonly in north and west Scotland, but a regular autumn and winter visitor along the east coast, probably from Scandinavia.

[137]

Blakeney Point, Norfolk 15.15–18.45

Two Arctic Skuas flew past east, more Sandwich Terns and 30 Brent Geese flew west.

One juvenile Long-tailed Skua came low along the shore from west landing on the sea just offshore. After a while took off and flew off east.

Not a great deal bigger than nearby Sandwich Tern; graceful flight action with wings held angled, light and easy with none of the heavy-chested, 'shouldery' appearance of Arctic Skua. Rather piebald plumage with darkish brown upper-wings, tail and cap contrasting with creamy collar and under-parts. Face, flanks, and vent finely barred brownish, under-wings finely barred grey. Minimal white wing patches, and creamy tipped upper-tail coverts forming a distinct U-shaped rump-patch. Bluey-grey legs and feet visible when landing on the sea.

Long-tailed Skua. A scarce, mostly autumn, passage migrant from its northern European and Siberian breeding colonies, seen annually in some numbers in recent years.

There appeared to have been a small fall along the point, with 100+ Goldcrests in Sueda belt and plantation, also several Song Thrushes, 5+ Willow Warbler/Chiffchaffs, 3 Wheatears, 2 Blackcaps, 2 Redstarts, 1 Whinchat and 1 Garden Warbler in the sparse cover.

One Barn Owl hovering over roadside allotments, under street lights in Thetford.

[138]

Redisham, Suffolk   09.30–11.15

The Roller seen immediately on arrival, and then watched for two hours, hunting from the roadside telegraph wires and exposed twigs and branches of fieldside trees, leaping down into fields from these vantage points and returning to nearby perches. A crippler of most obliging habits, allowing very close approach.

Very colourful plumage; pale turquoise-blue under-parts with greener head and rusty-buff wash on upper-breast, faded chestnut mantle and tertials, and vivid ultramarine and azure-blue wings, the black flight feathers showing a purple sheen below. At rest, golden-buff edgings to wing-coverts visible and narrow, slightly rounded tail showing very obscure dark spot at corners. Brown irides and pale brown feet also noted. Despite the exotic plumage, sometimes very difficult to locate when perched in the trees, but astonishingly vivid in flight.

Roller. Summer visitor to south and central Europe, but a rare vagrant to Britain, especially in recent years.

Two Woodcocks flew over main road outside Thetford in evening.

Davidstow Airfield, Cornwall   09.30–11.15

400+ Golden Plovers and 150+ Lapwings seen on disused airfield. The Baird's Sandpiper located feeding on turf near the road, with a single Dunlin. Similar in length to Dunlin, but structurally far smaller, a flat-looking bird with horizontal carriage and very long wings, with shortish, straight black bill and dark legs. Pale buff edgings to dark brown feathers giving a very fresh, scaly look to upper-parts. White below with well-defined pectoral band of brown striations. Dark eye-stripe, white supercilium and brown crown with a dark stripe extending down forehead to bill.

Flew off, calling—a triple, liquid 'prrik'.

Baird's Sandpiper. This 'weetabix-on-legs' is a rare transatlantic vagrant, mostly occurring in autumn. About 80 have been recorded in the British Isles.

Stithians Reservoir, Cornwall   14.10–15.40

One Pectoral Sandpiper feeding in shallow water beside the Golden Lion causeway. With a Dunlin for a while, when noted as being a little larger and longer-necked. A very neat bird with well-defined pectoral band and mantle-stripes. Dark cap, rusty ear-patch and yellowish legs noted.

Other waders here included 2 Curlew Sandpipers, 1 Common Sandpiper and 1 Knot.

500+ Golden Plovers near southern causeway, thoroughly checked—mostly juveniles and some moulting and winter plumage adults, but bewildering plumage variation between individuals on close scrutiny, including some grey birds, some with buffy under-parts and 1 very small, pale (aberrant?) bird.

Very little of interest seen on the Hayle estuary, St. Just, or Porth-gwarra, except 1 Manx Shearwater flying west at the last.

Marazion Marsh, Cornwall   08.15–18.45

A brief visit produced several Water Rails and 1 Spotted Crake disappearing into the reeds, the latter showing rich buff under-tail coverts, and 1 Sedge Warbler.

THE SCILLIES

A few Gannets, Kittiwakes and Razorbills seen from the *Scillonian*, also 1 Sooty Shearwater flying west low over a calm sea. Five *alba* Wagtails flew over the boat. Twelve or perhaps more Pilot Whales, in several small parties, provided a bonus.

St. Mary's   12.30–14.00

Two Pied Flycatchers, 3+ Willow Warbler/Chiffchaffs and 2 Reed Warblers seen on Lower Moors. One Yellow-browed Warbler located immediately in sallows beside the track, with a second bird calling nearby. Small, very attractive warbler, with bright olive-green upperparts and white under-parts, long yellow supercilium and double yellowy wing-bars. Clean white edges to tertials, and fine white tips to all secondaries and primaries noted.

Call most distinctive—a far-carrying, plaintive 'weesp .

A brief look around Rocky Hills area produced 2+ Whinchats, 1 Redstart, 5+ Stonechats and 1 semi-Hooded Crow.

Yellow-browed Warbler. Very scarce, though regular, autumn passage migrant from Siberia, mostly on the east coast but also on Scillies.

St. Agnes   15.05–16.30

The immature Yellow-billed Cuckoo watched in the trees overhanging the lane at the Parsonage, running along branches, flitting between trees and eating several small, juicy caterpillars. Watched from just a few yards' range, often sitting still for long periods with wings drooped and tail cocked, looking around for prey with slow, deliberate head turning. Missing a few tail feathers, but otherwise plumage quite neat; soft-grey crown and nape, slightly darker cheeks, mid-brown upper-parts with darker wings with large bright rufous patch on flight-feathers, and silky-white under-parts. Tail long and graduated, the feathers edged and tipped with white. Bill relatively long and decurved at tip, bright yellow with most of upper mandible (and very tip of lower) dark grey-brown, and prominent eye-ring lemon yellow. Brown irides and blue-grey legs and feet noted.

Yellow-billed Cuckoo. North America. Very rare vagrant in autumn, few seem to survive the transatlantic flight—38 have been recorded here.

St. Mary's   17.00–19.00

Immature Red-backed Shrike perched on telegraph wires beside road near Lower Moors. Quite a heavily marked bird—dark mask, scaly above with cream-edged coverts and crescentic barring on under-parts.

One Whinchat and 30+ Wheatears around the edge of the golf-course. One Yellow Wagtail dashing around on turf, showing very grey plumage with white underparts, but thin supercilium and wing-bars and buff wash on flanks.

Two Lapland Buntings running along furrows in ploughed field, and on fairway—dark corners to ear coverts and rufous wing coverts noted.

Other birds here included 50+ Meadow Pipits, several Stonechats, and 1 Whimbrel on putting green.

St. Mary's   07.15–10.00

One Pied Flycatcher on pavement near Lower Moors.

The immature Rose-coloured Starling seen rather briefly several times near the golf club-house, flying around with Starlings, occasionally landing on the fairway and in pine trees. Distinctly different in shape to Starling, being shorter and stouter-bodied with shorter, broader bill and big feet. Paler overall, biscuit-coloured with buffy rump and pale under-parts.

One White and 2 Yellow Wagtails, and 5+ Wheatears on golf-course, 3 Willow Warbler/Chiffchaffs, 1 Reed Warbler, 1 Whinchat and 1 Pied Flycatcher along Lower Moors.

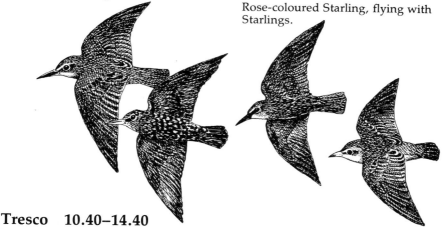

Rose-coloured Starling, flying with Starlings.

Tresco   10.40–14.40

Two Lapland Buntings flew up from meadow on hillside, calling—characteristic flat, toneless 'tc trrk k'.

One ♀ Red-backed Shrike perched on fencewire along edge of same field—a relatively plain bird, only lightly marked on under-parts. Also several Stonechats and Rock Pipits, 1 White and 2 Grey Wagtails here. At the Great Pool, 3 Dunlins, 1 Curlew Sandpiper, 2+ Greenshanks and 4 Common Sandpipers were feeding on mud along the edge of the reed-beds.

[145]

One Lesser Yellowlegs watched preening, and wading around in small bay. An excellent bird, finely proportioned with long deep yellow-orange legs and feet, fine black bill. Perhaps darker-mantled, a little browner, than the Drift bird, though upper-parts liberally spangled with white, silvery underparts with greyer breast. One Pectoral Sandpiper picked up in flight, then seen later feeding in muddy bay. Typically, a well marked bird with pale mantle lines and sharp pectoral band, feeding with hunched carriage on flexed legs.

Pectoral Sandpiper and (flying) Lesser Yellowlegs, two of the American waders most likely to be seen in Britain.

Many Gadwall, Mallard and Teal on pool; also 5 Shovelers, 1 Pintail and 2 Wigeon.

The ♂ Ring-necked Duck was floating around with a raft of about 20 Pochard, mostly asleep, though put head up briefly to show characteristic blue and white banded bill and yellow eye. Plumage pattern as adult ♂, but overall brownish cast to body and head, with ashy-brown smoked flanks.

Migrants seen around the Great Pool included many Goldcrests, a very fine Firecrest, 6+ Willow Warbler/Chiffchaffs, 2 Blackcaps and 4 Garden Warblers. Also seen were 2 Ravens flying over and 1 Water Rail, a juvenile, clambering around up in a sycamore tree.

Ring-necked Duck. Another individual to add to the recent run of records of this formerly incredibly rare American duck.

St. Mary's 15.40–18.50

Four sub-adult Kittiwakes in Hugh Town harbour.

Migrants seen in the evening included 1 Pied Flycatcher, 1 Tree Pipit and 2+ Wheatears, on the airport, and all that was seen at Porthellick was 1 Grey Wagtail, 2 Water Rails and 1 Heron, the latter eating with some difficulty a very large eel.

NNE5 *October 4* sunny

St. Mary's 07.40–13.30

Ten or more Wheatears on the golf-course.

The immature Rose-coloured Starling finally seen well, watched at close range feeding in rough turf along the edge of the fairway, and proving to be a super bird.

Relatively pale pinky-buff overall with slightly darker brown crown and ear coverts, plain brown mantle with darker wings (especially primaries) and tail, slightly paler rump. Wings showing a pale upper wing-bar and silvery-buff edges and tips to greater coverts and secondaries. Paler under-parts, white on chin and throat, with subtle buffy-grey mottling on breast and buffish flanks and under-tail coverts. Legs and feet pink, shortish bill pale yellowy/horn-coloured with pale brown culmen, eye dark.

With its large feet, high-stepping gait and head held high and bobbed, the bird gave a rather comic impression.

Rose-coloured Starling. Breeds in SE Europe and SW Asia, often wandering and sometimes invading southern Europe in some numbers. A rare vagrant to Britain, usually in late summer.

[147]

One Wryneck perched on top of telegraph pole, sunbathing, at Porth-loo. Watched lazily picking at lichen on the pole and then flew down into garden where it hopped around base of hedge. A typical intricately marked bird, very broad-winged in flight with rounded tail, when the grey rump contrasting with dark mantle stripe quite distinctive.

Migrants along Lower Moors included 3 Blackcaps, 1 Pied Flycatcher, 1 Whinchat and several Reed Warblers and Willow Warbler/Chiffchaffs.

One or two Firecrests seen flitting around in trees near Old Town, located by call—a sharp, repeated 'Zeet'.

One Richard's Pipit flushed from rough grass along edge of airfield, then grilled feeding, out on area of short turf—a large, long-legged, long-tailed pipit with stout bill and heavily streaked mantle. Broad creamy supercilium fading out, downcurved, behind cheek. Dark eye-stripe and streaked crown, rich brown ear-coverts and heavy black moustachial. White under-parts with buff breast, heavily spotted with black, and flanks streaked more finely. All wing-feathers dark brown broadly edged off-white and buff, especially coverts and tertials. Dark tail with prominent white outer-feathers. Large bill pink with brown

Richard's Pipit. A scarce vagrant from Asia, normally occurring annually in late autumn.

upper mandible and tip, very long legs orangy-flesh, the hind toes equipped with very long, curved claw.

Distinctive call heard several times in flight—a flat, dry House Sparrow-like chirp, slightly drawn-out and lacking the 'rolling' quality of Tawny Pipit—monotone 'chuurp' or 'shuurp'.

Also on the airfield were 2 Wheatears, and 1 Greenshank was in Old Town Bay.

Two Ring Ouzels seen on Peninnis Head—1 very scaly juvenile perched on stone wall, and a darker female in gorse patch. Also, 1 Lapland Bunting flew over, calling.

St. Agnes 14.45–15.45
One Yellow Wagtail feeding on tennis-court.

One Red-breasted Flycatcher watched flitting around in dead tree at the edge of the Parsonage, calling—a short, soft Wren-like rattle. Typically, a small, dumpy bird with drooped wings and nervously cocked tail, in typical rather nondescript autumn plumage; mousy-brown above and creamy-white below with buff wash on breast. Darker wings showing very slightly paler-edged coverts and narrow orangy wing-bar. Short blackish tail with white basal panels, occasionally visible when tail flicked, but very prominent in flight. Beady eye framed in pale buff orbital ring, short legs and bill black.

Red-breasted Flycatcher. Mostly a scarce though regular autumn migrant, primarily seen on the east coast.

[149]

October 5

St. Mary's

Very few migrants seen—only 5 Wheatears, 8+ Willow Warbler/Chiff-chaffs, 2 Blackcaps, 1 Tree Pipit, 1 Pied Flycatcher, 1 Redstart and 1 Sand Martin were perhaps worthy of note. Also several Swallows, House Martins, 2 Whimbrels, and 3 Stock Doves seen.

October 6

St. Mary's

A quick look at Porthellick revealed 2 Greenshanks and 1 Yellow Wagtail, but the rest of the day was spent indoors, due to the high wind.

October 7

St. Mary's

Again too windy for me, the only birds noted being 4+ Greenshanks, and the most obliging Lesser Yellowlegs at Lower Moors. This bird could be watched at just a few yards' range on the small pool in front of hide, allowing a thorough scrutiny of the intricately patterned grey, white and brown plumage, strong white eye-ring and pale line from eye to bill. Incredibly long deep yellow legs and slim build noted—it seemed to have some difficulty keeping a foothold in the strong wind, often being blown sideways and staggering to remain upright!

Lesser Yellowlegs. Presumably the same individual that was on Tresco—a rather brownish mantled individual which spent much of the rest of the month at Porthellick.

[150]

St. Mary's

The excellent Lesser Yellowlegs seen again on Lower Moors, feeding actively and often disappearing into reed-filled ditches.

One Yellow-browed Warbler seen flitting through sallow bushes in reeds besides track. A very 'clean' bird, but with a rather ill-defined upper wing-bar, but showing bright green wing and tail panels and white tips to all flight feathers. Called once. Other migrants along Lower Moors included 1 ♂ Redstart, 1 Pied Flycatcher, 1 Firecrest and 3+ Reed Warblers, one of the latter showing a greyish cast to upper-parts (especially head) and yellowy feet.

One ♂ Bluethroat watched feeding under bushes beside track, grovelling amongst dead leaves and perching on low dead branches. Very Robin-like in actions, running and stopping suddenly, with puffed-out shape and constantly flicking tail high up over back. Retaining much colour on breast; broad bright blue band across chest extending forward as black moustachials, and bordered below with a chestnut band.

Bluethroat. Autumn birds can show a great variety of patterning on the breast.

One immature Barred Warbler leaping clumsily around in bushes at the end of Watermill Lane, often sitting motionless for long periods. Very bulky warbler, generally grey-looking with pale edged tertials and secondaries, but perhaps poorly defined wing-bars. Other birds seen during the day included another Pied Flycatcher, 1 Spotted Flycatcher and 1 Garden Warbler. Also seen were 1 Golden Plover, 1 Greenshank, and a small juvenile Ringed Plover on the beach at Porthellick, showing dull flesh-coloured legs, extensive pale forehead and supercilium, paler mantle with pale-edged wing coverts and calling with a non-ringing 'chu lit'.

NW4	_October 9_	sunny periods

St. Agnes
One Firecrest moving through trees at the Parsonage, with quick, acrobatic feeding technique, while other migrants included 1 Redstart, 1 Yellow Wagtail, 20 Swallows and 1 Redwing.

Ten Golden Plovers and 1 Sanderling feeding on exposed seaweed.

One immature ♂ Merlin dashed across northern end of island, low over hedgerows—very small and quick, showing a mixture of characters—bluey mantle and tail, latter with blackish barring and a broad subterminal band, brownish primaries and strong face-pattern.

Firecrest, Pied Flycatcher and Redstart, typical passage migrants which may be seen virtually daily during the autumn on Scillies.

Merlin. Breeds in suitable moorland habitat in much of northern and western Britain, dispersing in the winter, when numbers are seen at coastal sites.

St. Mary's
No sign of the Rosefinch at Pelistry, and few other migrants besides 1 Whinchat, 1 White Wagtail and 1 Firecrest at Holy Vale.

St. Mary's
The Lesser Yellowlegs seen to fly from Lower Moors, over Old Town. Perhaps more migrants in evidence today—5 Whinchats, 1 Redstart, 10+ Willow Warbler/Chiffchaffs, 2 Yellow Wagtails, 3 Turtle Doves, 1 Whitethroat, 1 Pied Flycatcher and several House Martins noted in Lower Moors and Holy Vale.

Despite checking various fields holding flocks of Linnets, House Sparrows and Goldfinches, still no sign of the Rosefinch, but 1 Bluethroat flew up from one such field at Pelistry, landing on a large cabbage leaf and fanning tail to show bright chestnut basal panels, and turning to show supercilium, moustachial stripes and dark breast-band.

Other birds seen during the day included the usual Swallows and Grey Wagtails, 1 Snipe and the resident semi-Hooded Crow.

Another Bluethroat, possibly an immature or female.

[153]

St. Mary's
One Merlin, three Whinchats and 1 Spotted Flycatcher at Salakee.

Red-eyed Vireo. North America, wintering South America. Only the 8th record in Britain of this transatlantic vagrant. All in autumn, five have been on Scillies.

One Red-eyed Vireo seen feeding in lower part of hedge above the quarry at Porthellick House. Watched in bright sunshine in this, just about the only, sheltered spot on the island! A totally hyperzonky megacrippler, perhaps reminiscent of a giant Firecrest. In size possibly a little larger than Garden Warbler, and often appearing pot-bellied with a broad, flat head. Upper-parts golden-green, extending as a smudge on the 'shoulders', with darker bronzy-olive wings and tail. Under-parts silky-white with a clear lemon-yellow wash on the vent area and under-tail coverts. Head pattern most striking—bluey-grey crown bordered on either edge by a black stripe, long white supercilium (narrow at bill and flaring out behind eye) and black eye-stripe above green ear-coverts. Rather heavy dark-edged pale bill, strong grey legs and feet, and deep wine-red irides noted.

Though moving very quickly between bushes, appeared rather lethargic while feeding, adopting Hippo-like actions to pick up caterpillars which were beaten on the branch before being swallowed. The clean, fresh plumage and yellow vent suggest a juvenile bird.

St. Agnes 10.15
A few migrants, including 1 Yellow-browed Warbler, several Redwings and a Siskin, and a party of 8 Great Tits headed out to sea from Gugh.

Isabelline Shrike. A summer visitor to southern Asia, this is only the 16th individual to be recorded in Britain.

The Isabelline Shrike was located hunting from the hedges around the small fields on Gugh.

Seemed to be similar in shape to Red-backed Shrike, with a very slightly graduated tail. Very pale overall appearance—olivy-grey/buff above and off-white below—combined with orangy tail giving a distinctly Redstart-like look. Wings darker than mantle with tertiaries and secondaries broadly edged buff forming a strong pale wing panel. Richer honey-brown mask behind the large dark eye and pale supercilium flaring out behind eye noted. Tail, though generally orangy, showing less bright olivy-tinged central feathers (and tips to others) and pale-edged outer-feathers, but rump and upper-tail coverts clean, bright orange. Pale horn-pink bill (with browner culmen and tip) and pale feet also noted.

[155]

St. Mary's 12.45

One Melodious Warbler feeding at top of hedge at Salakee, occasionally perching on telegraph wires. A typical Hippo, stoutly built with a long pale bill and greyish legs. Showing distinctive combination of very short wings (with no pale panel), steep forehead but rounded crown and large, dark eye. A very pale, greyish-buff-coloured individual.

Two Whinchats in cabbage field beside track.

One ♀/immature Scarlet Rosefinch watched in and around this field, perched on hedgerow bracken and brambles, and feeding on weeds amongst the crop.

A very neat, slim, slightly top-heavy looking bird, a little longer than Linnet with round head and conical bill. Rather nondescript plumage; subtly streaked olivy mantle and rump, darker tail and wings, latter showing clear, narrow double wing-bars and pale edged tertials (though all tail and wing-feathers with very narrow paler edgings), and off-white under-parts with brownish streaking on throat and breast. Virtually featureless buffy-coloured head, slightly darker on crown and cheeks, with large dark Teddy-bear-button eyes. Brownish legs and feet, grey-brown bill.

No further sign of the Vireo at Porthellick House, but 1 Blackcap and 1 Firecrest seen, the latter a very bright bird with bronzy 'cape' and deep orange crown—presumably a male.

Scarlet Rosefinch. Summer visitor to NE Europe; a rare though annual autumn visitor to Britain, mostly on Shetlands.

[156]

St. Agnes   08.30

The Booted Warbler seen virtually immediately, in crops and in tamarisk bushes near the old observatory. Though obviously a Hippo (long-billed and bulky), very small—even shorter in length than nearby Chiffchaffs. First impressions of a generally pale grey-brown bird with darker tail (vaguely reminiscent of Desert Warbler?).

Quite pot-bellied with steep forehead to peaked crown, quite long wings and longish, notched tail. Overall cold grey-brown above, darker on forehead and rear ear-coverts, with thin off-white supercilium, wider and fading behind the eye, and inconspicuous dark eye-stripe. Under-parts off-white with a pale buffy wash on sides of upper breast, throat pure white. Fairly dark brown wings, all flight feathers edged paler but broad whitish edges to tertials and secondaries forming a distinct pale panel on closed wing. Dark tail tinged chestnut-brown with narrow whitish outer webs to outer-tail feathers, quite conspicuous when tail flicked in shadow but hardly visible at any other time. Quite long, thin bill pale brown with darker culmen, and stout legs pale grey-brown in colour.

Booted Warbler. A summer visitor to central Asia, this is the 11th ever to be recorded in Britain and only the 4th outside Shetlands.

Other migrants on the island included Whinchat, several Redwings and Willow Warbler/Chiffchaffs and 1 Merlin (flying across the bay from Gugh very speedily, on flicked, half-closed wings).

The Isabelline Shrike watched again on Gugh; far more active than on last occasion, adopting a much more streamlined pose. Inconspicuous silvery-buff scalloping noted on upper flanks and breast, extending forward as a barely discernible moustachial. These markings, which presumably indicate a juvenile, were visible only at close range.

[157]

St. Mary's   14.00

One Yellow-browed Warbler located by call—a whispery (but penetrating) 'sweet' and watched flitting through sallow bushes beside Lower Moors nature trail.

Also here were 6+ Willow Warblers/Chiffchaffs, the same moulting ♂ Redstart and 1 Firecrest in copse by bridge (but feeding too close to focus bins—the supercilium plainly visible without optical aid).

One Hooded Crow flew overhead, calling.

Several Water Rails squealing from the reed-beds, 1 bird creeping nervously along on the footpath.

Another Richard's Pipit watched feeding on short turf on the airfield. A very confiding bird, but completely different from the first bird in plumage and with actions more often associated with Tawny Pipit—*flava*-wagtail type runs and stops and frequent tail-wagging, usually adopting a relatively horizontal carriage. Also appeared slightly smaller with a less stout bill than the first bird, and certainly less heavily marked with neatly streaked mantle, vestigial moustachial and fine streaks on upper breast (and to a lesser extent on flanks). However, otherwise quite dark, with a rich buff wash on breast, and characteristic buff surround to the eye giving the bird a rather 'stary' expression. Long yellowy-pink legs and long hind claw noted, and in flight showed a very dark tail with white outer-feathers. Called several times—the distinctive monotonous 'chuurp'.

Also several Wheatears on runway, and 1 very tame Whimbrel stalking around nearby—kinked bill, crown stripes and bright lead-blue legs and feet noted.

Whimbrel. Mainly a passage migrant, when it is often found in coastal meadows and mudflats.

St. Mary's

One ♂ Ring Ouzel flushed from track at Lower Moors, calling, showing characteristic grey wings contrasting with scaly black body.

One Ortolan Bunting located hopping around near the lighthouse on Peninnis Head, sheltering behind grass clumps and apparently feeding on heather seeds. In basic plumage resembling a washed-out adult—-head olivy-grey with slightly darker, streaked, forehead and lores, off-white throat, yellowish malar stripe and white eye-ring. Upper-parts olivy-chestnut, streaked dark brown, with pale pinky-grey lines down either side of mantle. Wings blackish brown with prominent double wing-bars, broad goldeny edges to tertials and narrower pale edges to secondaries and greater coverts. Under-parts generally orangy-pink, sandier on breast, with dark moustachial and gorget of brown streaks. Compact pink bill and pale pinkish legs noted.

Ortolan Bunting. A scarce annual spring and, more commonly, autumn visitor. Though generally regarded as a drift migrant, it seems likely that the later birds occurring in south-west Britain are of southern origin.

St. Mary's

Little time spent in the field due to adverse weather conditions, though migrants on Peninnis included 1 Whinchat, several Willow Warbler/Chiffchaffs and 5+ Wheatears, one of the latter a large pale bird with heavy bill and broad sandy edgings on wing.

The Ortolan seen again, sheltering from the gale on Peninnis Head—a rather bleak site which the bird appeared to prefer to the sheltered weedy fields nearby. Flew, calling—a soft, liquid 'quik', and showing white outer tail feathers and streaked, warm brown, rump.

St. Mary's

Jack Snipe, a shy and solitary winter
visitor from Northern Europe and
Siberia.

One Jack Snipe watched on pool just in front of hide at Lower Moors,
and feeding with characteristic rhythmical bobbing action, often very
exaggerated, the body moving up and down apparently independently
of the legs. A smashing dumpy, tail-less-looking bird, very richly
patterned above with green and purple gloss on feathers, prominent
creamy mantle stripes and double supercilium. Relatively short,
broad-based bill, and large dark eye, set well back in head, noted.

About 10 Fieldfares and 50 Redwings feeding on berry-laden
hawthorn bushes at Holy Vale.

One Icterine Warbler feeding in ivy-covered trees near Holy Vale
farmhouse in typical lethargic manner, jumping about rather clumsily
and stretching out to snap up convenient flies. Generally very pale
warbler, olivy-grey/buff above and whitish below with yellowish wash
on upper breast. Distinctive features included the very long wings (the
primary tips progressively widely spaced) with pale wing panel, rather
shallow forehead to peaked crown and relatively small-looking eye.
Long, stout pale brown bill and strong bluey-grey legs noted. One ♀
Pied Flycatcher also feeding in these ivy-covered trees, in a far more
active style, dashing among the trunks to catch flies with a clearly
audible snap of the bill.

[160]

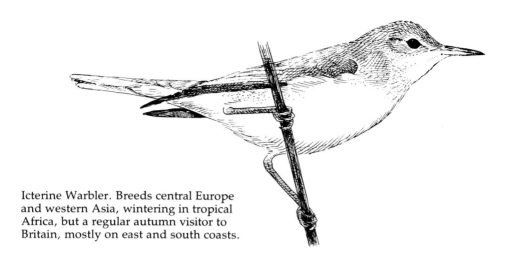

Icterine Warbler. Breeds central Europe and western Asia, wintering in tropical Africa, but a regular autumn visitor to Britain, mostly on east and south coasts.

One Red-breasted Flycatcher watched in Holy Vale, feeding in a sheltered area of trees beside the track. Plumage basically similar to the St. Agnes bird—mousy-brown above and off-white below with pale eye-ring—but less clean-looking, and showing a slight pale panel on the closed wing. Short black tail with distinctive white panels showing to good effect when hovering to pick insects from the bark of trees.

Many Goldcrests and 10+ Willow Warbler/Chiffchaffs here; also 30+ Swallows and 1 House Martin.

At Porthellick Pool the Lesser Yellowlegs was feeding in the back edge, in front of reed-bed. Later seen standing alongside a group of 5 Greenshanks, preening, when the small size, silvery appearance and disproportionately long orange-yellow legs were particularly evident.

Three Teal feeding on pool.

Other migrants seen included 1 Whinchat and the tame Whimbrel at Salakee, 1 Golden Plover on the airfield, and perhaps far fewer Linnets, most of the usual fields rather empty of birds.

Red-breasted Flycatcher.

[161]

St. Mary's

One Richard's Pipit feeding on the airfield in the same area as the last bird, but a different individual assuming a more characteristic upright, leggy, stance and hardly ever wagging tail. Upper-parts similarly marked to the previous bird, but showing strong triple 'v' pattern formed by broad pale borders to tertials, and well-defined broad super-cilium, lacking the buff eye-surround. Under-parts creamy-coloured, with only a large blackish smudge on moustachial/upper breast.

One ♀ Merlin flew up over airfield, turning and heading back to Salakee with relatively lazy flight-manner, obviously not hunting. Seen to be dark chocolate-brown above, with heavy blotched head and chest and dark barring on under-wings.

The Lesser Yellowlegs was feeding as usual at Porthellick, along with Greenshank, Whimbrel, 3 Snipe and 3 Teal.

One ♀ Goldeneye on the pool, diving just near hide, showing 'triangular' dark-brown head, greyish body and white collar and wing patch.

The juvenile Icterine Warbler seen again, high in the trees by farm-house. The Red-breasted Flycatcher in Holy Vale, was sitting still for long periods, when appeared totally spherical but for projecting bill and narrow wings with the white panels in tail obscured by under-tail coverts when viewed from below. Other migrants seen during the day included 3 Blackcaps, 10+Swallows, 10+ Willow Warbler/Chiffchaffs, 100+ Redwings, several Fieldfares and Wheatears, and 2 Bramblings.

Meadow Pipits (50+) and 17 Skylarks were on Peninnis, where the Ortolan Bunting was flitting around, drenched, after a heavy rainstorm; wing-bars and tail spots noticeable in flight. Called several times—a loud, squeaky 'pweik'.

Two of the four Richard's Pipits seen during the month, showing variation in plumage between today's bird (right) and the individual on 19th. Also compare bird on 4th.

[162]

Northern Chiffchaff, probably the
Siberian race, a rare late autumn visitor,
similar in appearance to the more regular
Scandinavian race.

St. Mary's

A short sea-watch from Peninnis Lighthouse produced 50+ Gannets,
100+ Kittiwakes, 5 Guillemots and 1 Fulmar, all flying south-west.

The Ortolan was seen again on the headland, and the Richard's Pipit
was still present on the airfield.

One Chiffchaff in the gorse beside the stone wall on Peninnis was a
particularly pale bird, very pale sandy brown above and white below,
with buff wash on sides of breast and flanks and black legs. These
features, plus the plaintive 'sweee' call, indicate that it was probably of
the Siberian race *tristis*.

The Red Kite seen flying over Rocky Hills; though rather distant,
easily identified by large size, contrasting wing pattern and long forked
orangy tail.

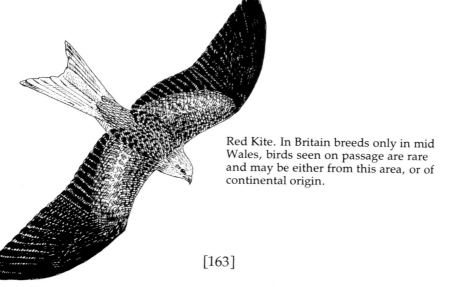

Red Kite. In Britain breeds only in mid
Wales, birds seen on passage are rare
and may be either from this area, or of
continental origin.

[163]

Tresco   10.30–16.30

The resident ♀ Black Duck seen standing on seaweed-covered rocks offshore near the Old Quay, with 1 ♂ Mallard. A very dark-looking duck with mottled blackish-brown body, paler buffy head and neck with darker crown and eye-stripe. Dark purplish speculum, bordered at rear with a fine white line, visible on closed wing. Dull yellowy-green bill and orangy legs also noted.

♀ Black Duck with ♂ Mallard. Only 11 have been recorded in the British Isles, but this bird has been present since October 1976.

One Richard's Pipit flew past on hilltop, calling—the usual distinctive loud 'schuurp'. Seen in flight to be large and long-tailed with dark brown-streaked plumage and dark tail with contrasting white outer-feathers. Seen only briefly on ground before flying off across the island (though it was apparently seen again near the Old Quay).

A few migrants around the hillside included 60+ Swallows, 1 Black Redstart, 1 Turtle Dove, and many small parties of Chaffinches moving over.

One Olive-backed Pipit watched feeding in the edge of grassy field near the Great Pool, occasionally flying up into overhanging trees to preen. Typical feeding method, pushing through and under vegetation with mole-like persistence—the movement of the grass often being the only indication as to its progress. When in the open the bird was constantly wagging its tail in a slow, almost involuntary, manner.

[164]

Olivy-brown on mantle and crown, fairly well streaked, with a uniform olive rump. Wings darker than mantle with warm-buff edges to tertials and coverts, latter tipped paler to form indistinct double wing-bars. Longish tail dark, with white outer-feathers (showing especially at tips). Most distinctive head-pattern–strong buffy-white supercilium bordered above by dark stripe along edge of crown and below by dark eye-stripe, this running up to separate the supercilium from the off-white supercilium 'drop', this in turn contrasting with the dark cheek-spot. Warm-buff ear-coverts and rather plain area between bill and eye also noted. Under-parts white with buff wash over breast, marked with black moustachial and heavy black streaking on breast, finer on flanks. Fairly stout purplish-brown bill and pinkish-brown legs also noted.

Olive-backed Pipit. Only the 13th record in Britain of this skulking pipit from central Asia.

On the Great Pool were 6 Wigeon (including an immature bird which appeared longer and lower in the water, and showing a greyish, rather angular head and pinkish flanks, vaguely reminiscent of American Wigeon). The ♂ Ring-necked Duck was still present, sleeping with a raft of 40 Pochard and 3 Tufted Ducks. Three Pintail, 10 Shovelers and 1 Greenshank also seen.

W4 _____*October 23*_____ cloudy

Tresco 10.30
Much the usual birds on the Great Pool, including 50+ Teal, 35 Pochard, 3 Tufted Ducks, 3 Pintail and several Shovelers.
Three ♀-plumaged Goldeneye were on the water, and 1 Greenshank feeding nearby.

A flock of 13 White-fronted Geese flew over, calling, and other migrants included 4 Black Redstarts around the Barn Flats and 1 pale Chiffchaff in the sallows beside the Great Pool, greyish above and off-white below (probably of the Scandinavian race *abietinus*).

St. Mary's 16.45

One Red-rumped Swallow flying around gardens and sea-wall at Porthcressa beach, perching for long periods on telephone wires between the houses, allowing for protracted grilling.

Neat blackish cap and mantle glossed with a metallic-blue sheen, wings blue-black with browner primaries and showing creamy-white tips to tertials and inner greater coverts. Upper-tail and under-tail coverts black, and tail (with shorter, broader streamers than nearby Swallows) also black in colour. Rump and under-parts creamy-white, latter with buff wash across breast, merging into extensive orangy collar. Cheek rather darker and a rufous-red stripe noted between the eye and cap. In flight the under-wings showed as dull grey-brown with buffish orange coverts.

Decidedly House Martin-like in flight at dusk, when the fairly blunt wings and shortish tail streamers, combined with the black and off-white plumage (the orangy areas being inconspicuous in poor light) could be quite deceiving.

Red-rumped Swallow. Formerly much rarer, this vagrant (from south and east Eurasia and Africa) has now been recorded annually in the last 15 years.

St. Mary's 10.00

The Red-rumped Swallow watched again, hawking back and forth along the shoreline of Littleporth with several Swallows. More lethargic flight action noted, often 'parachuting' up over the bushes on the Garrison. Showing less metallic sheen on upper-parts than the Swallows, and less broad wing-base, with the orange face and collar and upper-rump noticeable at some distance.

One Black Redstart seen on the beach here, another at Old Town.

One Brambling seen on Peninnis, in weedy field along with 50+ Chaffinches, 50+ Linnets and several Greenfinches and Goldfinches.

One Snow Bunting flew overhead towards the airfield.

One ♀ Merlin hunting over the field behind Old Town was seen again chasing finches at Higher Moors—a fairly lightly marked bird with dull ashy-brown upper-parts. One Lapland Bunting flew over the edge of the airfield, calling, near Giant's Castle.

Black Redstart. Passage migrant with birds present daily through most of the month on Scillies. Large numbers appeared in the last week with up to 20 birds on Porthloo beach alone.

The Lesser Yellowlegs flew in to Porthellick pool, feeding actively for a short while along the muddy edges before disappearing into the reeds.

Two Firecrests and 1 Yellow-browed Warbler were seen together in bushes beside the track, the latter showing a rather dull olive mantle, greyish-olive mid-crown band, and grey wash on breast. Wing-bars and supercilium were quite bright though, the wings also showing a bright green panel on the secondaries.

Among migrants at Holy Vale were 25+ Swallows, 12+ Willow Warbler/Chiffchaffs (including one pale, *abietinus*-type Chiffchaff) and 1 late Reed Warbler, while among the winter birds were 1 Brambling and 50+ Redwings.

The Icterine Warbler was seen again, feeding in the usual tall trees near Holy Vale Farmhouse.

October on the Scillies is never complete without its annual controversy, on this occasion a small Whitethroat-like *Sylvia* on Peninnis. Though I was in the Spectacled Warbler camp, the bird was trapped and established as being a Subalpine Warbler, presumably a juvenile.

Seen in the gorse near the lighthouse and, later, in brambles alongside the stone walls on the head, the initial impression was of a tiny Whitethroat with a relatively shorter tail.

Plumage a cold ashy-brown on mantle and rump with darker wings, the latter showing broad dull-brown edges to coverts and quite bright rufous-buff edges to all flight feathers, broadest and brightest on secondaries/tertials but not forming a complete wing panel. Head a little paler than mantle, greyish on crown and cheeks with a little sandy-brown showing on forehead and slightly darker around the eye. A small pale area noted between bill and eye, and narrow white eye-ring very obvious in the field, as was the apparently clear white throat. Underparts white with a fairly strong pinky-buff wash across breast and on flanks. Greyish tail showing obscure pale edges and tips to all feathers and very obvious white outer-feathers. Bill dull brown, darker on culmen and lower edge, and legs pale brown, even straw-coloured when viewed from behind, with very pale feet.

Subalpine Warbler. Summer visitor to the Mediterranean countries, wintering south of the Sahara. Occurs in Britain as a very rare vagrant in spring or autumn, virtually annually in recent years.

St. Martins

A visit on the strength of a rumoured Great Snipe produced very little besides 2 Ravens, 1 Buzzard (a dark bird with one tatty wing) and 1 Short-eared Owl, the latter flushed from heather-covered hillside showing typical blotchy upper-parts with large buff wing-flashes and heavily barred tail, and yellow eyes set in dark-centred facial discs. Two Snipe and 1 Blackcap also noted here.

St. Mary's

In the evening the Subalpine Warbler was still present on Peninnis and 1 Black Redstart seen at Old Town. The party of White-fronted Geese (seen on Tresco) flew over the airfield, but now consisting of only 12 birds.

St. Mary's

One Yellow-browed Warbler, located by call, flitting around in wind-blown twigs, high up in trees by Holy Vale farmhouse. Wing-bars and long supercilium noted, but a very dull individual.

Ten or more Chiffchaffs seen in Holy Vale.

One ♀/immature Scarlet Rosefinch feeding on weeds in small sheltered maize field at Salakee. A very clean bird, far less olivy than the bird on 12th, especially browner on mantle and wings. Otherwise plumage similar with standard thin but clear white wing-bars and pale edgings to tertials, fairly well streaked on mantle and on under-parts, where the markings continued up onto the throat. Characteristic chunky grey-brown bill and beady eye set in rather plain buffy-grey head noted, also grey legs.

One Blackcap and 1 late Whinchat still here, also 1 Black Redstart.

Sanderlings (50+) and 2 White Wagtails seen on Porthmellon Beach.

Scarlet Rosefinch. Though Shetland is the best place to see this vagrant, at least 2 birds were on Scillies during October and the species is perhaps to be expected here annually.

[169]

St. Mary's

One Long-eared Owl in bushes beside track at Lower Moors, located by cacophony of mobbing Robins, tits, thrushes and Chaffinches. Perched in rather open branches, in attenuated pose with raised ear-tufts, glaring fiercely around with deep orange eyes. Flew out across the road, landing first in roadside trees and then in evergreen hedge, its progress marked by its band of noisy followers. Delicately vermiculated plumage and finely barred tail noticeable in flight.

More than 10 Chiffchaffs seen along nature trail, 9 Snipe and 1 Heron feeding on small pool in front of the hide.

Several Siskins, 1 Black Redstart and 6+ Swallows seen at Hugh Town, and 1 Whimbrel over the golf course.

Long-eared Owl. Breeds locally in Britain but also a passage migrant with only one or two recorded on Scillies each year.

Olive-backed Pipit. A second individual, 5 of the 14 birds recorded have now been on Scillies.

One Olive-backed Pipit located feeding in weedy field behind pinewood at Macfarlands Down, near Bar Point. Watched at very close range though far less confiding than the Tresco bird, occasionally flying up into trees or hedges and once onto telegraph wires.

Called several times—'teezt', quite similar to Tree Pipit but a little more abrupt.

Distinctly cleaner-looking than the Tresco individual, the underparts and head completely lacking the buffish wash of that bird but for a restricted area of buff on the sides of breast. On the deck this bird was perhaps similar to a well-marked Tree Pipit but with distinctive head pattern—prominent white supercilium and cheek spot bordered by dark stripes and black spot on rear ear-coverts. Bare-looking loral area also noted. For its small size a rather bulky pipit with relatively stout bill and legs, the latter a curious purply-pink in colour.

October 29

St. Mary's

Raven. Resident in SW England, Wales and Scotland, in suitable hilly or coastal habitats.

[171]

One Raven flew over Rocky Hills, calling—'prook'.

One late Lesser Whitethroat in brambles alongside track, a very neat bird with dark mask and dark blue-grey legs.

One Yellow-browed Warbler and 1 Firecrest in the usual trees by Holy Vale farmhouse, and 1 late Willow Warbler seen on Higher Moors.

Other summer migrants included 10+ Chiffchaffs, 15+ Swallows and 1 Blackcap. Two Turtle Doves were still with about 30 Collared Doves in the stubble field at Salakee. Waders included 1 Whimbrel, 1 Greenshank and the Lesser Yellowlegs again on Porthellick pool.

Winter birds were represented by a distinct influx of thrushes, including several hundred Fieldfares and Redwings, 20+ Siskins and 1 Brambling.

One Siberian Stonechat watched flycatching from trees, wires and bracken around Porthloo duckpond—a very pale-looking bird overall with pale peach/apricot wash on under-parts, sharply demarcated pure white throat and white supercilia, meeting above the bill. Crown, cheeks and mantle and wing coverts grey-brown, rump and upper-tail coverts clear orange. Broad white edges to tertials and secondaries forming a strong pale wing panel, also white wing-bar and white inner-wing patch noted. Tail black, tipped pale.

One of the most striking features of the bird was the black 'armpits' in flight, very obvious due partly to the otherwise pale plumage and partly to its habit of indulging in frequent high-flying flycatching sallies.

Also of interest was a partial albino Wren.

Stonechat showing the characters of the eastern races (*S.t. maura* or *stejnegeri*). Colloquially called Siberian Stonechat, it is a rare vagrant to Britain, mostly in autumn.

[172]

Sandwich Bay, Kent

The Pallas's Warbler located in small clump of bushes in dunes by golf-course, providing excellent views feeding actively along the sheltered side of the bushes.

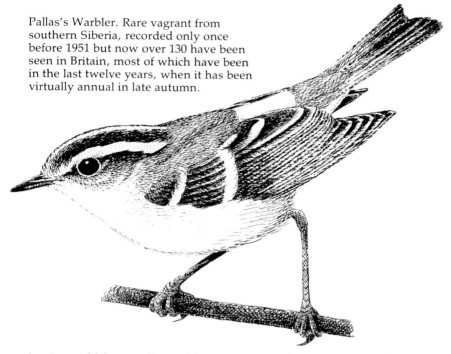

Pallas's Warbler. Rare vagrant from southern Siberia, recorded only once before 1951 but now over 130 have been seen in Britain, most of which have been in the last twelve years, when it has been virtually annual in late autumn.

An incredibly small warbler, more neatly proportioned than Goldcrest and even more restless, ceaselessly active and often hovering. As usual a jewel of a bird.

Bright olive-green above, silky white below with grey shoulder patches. Head with blackish crown with long yellow central stripe, long yellow supercilia over dark eye-stripes. Wings showing bright green panel, double yellow wing-bars and white edges to tertials. Neat square lower back/rump patch whitish, tinged lemon yellow towards upper edge, tail dark with bright green feather edgings. Relatively small brown bill, brown legs and dark eye noted. Often calling—a distinctive quiet, but far-carrying 'cheip', similar to the 'chiff' of Chiffchaff song.

Seen in hand later at the observatory (complete with brand new leg-iron), along with a Firecrest, when the neat proportions and fine bill made the Firecrest look disproportionately bulky!

Other birds seen here included 10+ Goldcrests and 50+ Golden Plovers.

[173]

Elmley Marshes (Sheppey), Kent

A flock of 500+ Golden Plovers in fields beside track. Many Wigeon, Shovelers, Teal, Gadwall and Pintail on reserve, also 60+ Greylag Geese and 2 adult Bewick's Swans, the latter up-ending in large pool on marsh and later preening on bank.

Apart from 200+ roosting Curlews, few other waders were seen except 3 Black-tailed Godwits and 1 Ruff.

One Hooded Crow flew along far edge of marsh, flushing many of the duck.

One ringtail Hen Harrier watched hanging in strong wind over reed-filled ditch near the car, showing very rusty under-parts and wing-linings, and clear-cut face-pattern—characters often associated with Montagu's Harrier.

November 8 ___ dull and misty

Waxham, Norfolk   14.30

The Pallas's Warbler was located, after some time, in the small copse behind the dunes, feeding in, and moving between, the oaks, these being the only trees here retaining any foliage. The plumage was noted as being basically very similar to the Sandwich Bay bird but perhaps a little cleaner-looking, darker olive-green above with a less-contrasting crown stripe but much brighter yellow wing-bars (the upper bar being quite pronounced) and with a richer yellow rump-patch.

Called only once, but as with the last bird a very distinctive 'cheip'.

Another Pallas's Warbler—a bird always pleasing to see, especially in the 'home' county.

[174]

Apart from a covey of about 30 Red-legged Partridges, little present in the wood except several Dunnocks, 1 Robin, 1+ Goldcrest and 1 excellent Firecrest. 60 Tree Sparrows and 1 Woodcock seen nearby.

November 9
misty, rain later

Crossbills. The most stable British breeding population appears to be in the Brecks, most other areas being only temporarily populated as a result of periodic irruptions of continental birds into Britain.

Holkham Pines (Wells end), Norfolk
Only a few Redwings, Fieldfares and Redpolls seen around the dell, also 1 Woodcock flushed from birch scrub. A party of 3 (2♂ 1♀) Crossbills flew over several times, calling—a most distinctive loud emphatic 'chip .... chip ....'. They landed in a nearby pine tree, the bright brick-red males singing, and then commenced feeding—silently but for the cracking of the pine-cones.

Cley, Norfolk
300+ Brent Geese seen grazing in the Eye field, also 750+ Wigeon, many Pintail and several Golden Plovers on reserve. On a brief seawatch many Kittiwakes and auks appeared to be moving east, far out, with 2 Guillemots and 1 Red-throated Diver on the sea close to the beach. One immature Little Gull flew along the shore.

Water Pipit. This continental, mountain-breeding, race of Rock Pipit is a regular winter visitor in small numbers, preferring freshwater habitats.

Salthouse, Norfolk   08.30

George, the regular Glaucous Gull, was on the marsh by the duck pond, preening, along with 10 Common and 50 Black-headed Gulls.

Twenty-two Shorelarks feeding around the pools on the shingle area behind the beach, showing distinctive yellow and black face-pattern and pale pinky-buff/grey upper-parts. Several flew, calling—whistling 'tsui' and 'tsee-seeo', showing sharply contrasting white under-parts and black tail-centre when banking.

Cley, Norfolk

One Water Pipit seen near Bittern Hide, a typically clean bird with virtually unmarked grey-brown upper-parts, white under-parts (neatly streaked) and white supercilium. Black legs and white outer-tail feathers also noted, and distinctive call—a short, sharp 'treek'.

Snow Bunting. Mainly a winter visitor to coastal areas, though in Scotland also in the highlands, where a few remain to breed on the high tops.

[176]

Holkham (W. Wood), Norfolk   11.00–13.00

Few birds seen besides 1 Firecrest, located by call, feeding in holm oaks near the house, and 1 late House Martin flying around the end of the wood.

Cley (E. bank to Salthouse), Norfolk   14.00–16.30

One late Greenshank flew across the reserve, calling, and 1 Red-breasted Merganser diving on Arnold's Marsh.

A party of 6 Snow Buntings watched feeding along the beach—very confiding birds, moving with shuffling and hopping gait, close to the ground. Individuals showing differing plumage patterns with varying amounts of mantle-streaking and head-colouring and more or less white in wing, but all with small, stout, orange bill and black legs.

Five Dunlins, 1 Grey Plover and 1 Brent Goose noted on the pools at Iron Road.

SW7 _____*November 17*_____ cloudy, drizzle later

Welney Wildfowl Refuge, Ouse Washes, Norfolk   09.00–12.00

Several small groups of Bewick's Swans flew across the river, calling, and about 30 seen later on lake in front of main hide.

A party of 6 Whooper Swans were out on the marsh—mostly sleeping but also preening and flying. Large size, very long neck and long bill with extensive yellow wedge (compared to the restricted yellow base of Bewick's) distinctive at any range.

Also hundreds of Wigeon, Shoveler and Teal, and a few Pintails, feeding out on marsh.

Pied Wagtails (2+) and 10+ Meadow Pipits around pool in front of Hide 51.

Whooper Swan. A winter visitor, most numerous in northern areas, and Bewick's Swan, also a winter visitor but with a more southerly distribution, the largest gatherings often being here at Welney, and at Slimbridge.

[177]

At 10.20, the Citrine Wagtail flew in from back of marshy area to land in close grass, then flew along close dyke to land on near muddy pool, where 'scoped before it ran into cover. Seen again several times, but only in flight and calling—a very distinctive loud, rather rasping 'tzzzp'. Crown, nape and mantle cold clear grey (the crown edged darker), darker wings with broad white double wing-bars and very broad white edges to tertials. Shortish, black, tail with strong white outer-feathers. Well-marked head-pattern, broad white supercilium, wider and slightly upcurved behind eye and merging into pale surround of the dark-bordered ear-coverts, the whole face washed with yellow.

Under-parts clear white but for blackish moustachial/throat smudge and gorget of diffuse dark spots across throat. Bill, eye and legs black.

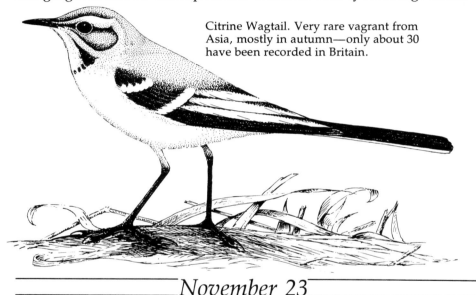

Citrine Wagtail. Very rare vagrant from Asia, mostly in autumn—only about 30 have been recorded in Britain.

November 23

Radipole Lake, Dorset   07.00–08.30

The immature Ring-billed Gull was located virtually immediately, standing on the mud by the car park, with several Common Gulls nearby for comparison.

Larger size and long wings noticed immediately, also 'meaner' expression (with squarer head-shape and dark 'mask') and far stouter bill, the latter pink with sharply demarcated blackish tip. Characteristic plumage noted—blackish-brown primaries and tertials contrasting with the pale grey mantle and secondaries and the dark brown wing-coverts with broad, convex, pale-buff edgings. Rather heavy brown spotting noted on flanks, belly and tail-coverts, and the dark tail bar broken along the upper edge, especially on outer-feathers.

Ring-billed Gull. Since the first record of this North American gull in 1973, over 30 have now been seen in Britain, mostly in the winter.

500+ Black-headed, 20+ Herring, 10+ Common and 5+ Great Black-backed Gulls were also standing around on the mud here, and 1 Greenshank feeding along the edge.

One Cetti's Warbler heard singing, and 1 juvenile Stonechat seen perched in the reeds near the road.

Staines Reservoir, Surrey   12.00

Among hundreds of Tufted Duck and Pochard, less usual ducks were represented by 1 ♂ Goosander and a party of 6 Goldeneye, diving close to the bank.

Lady Amherst's Pheasant. Introduced as an ornamental bird, this spectacular pheasant is now firmly established as a feral species.

[179]

Little Brickhill, Bucks   14.30

Two ♂ and 3 ♀ Lady Amherst's Pheasants stalked out, very warily, from area of young conifers, and watched feeding along forest ride.

The fabulous males spent most of the time feeding out on the track—handsome birds with black and white plumage and incredibly long tail. Black head, chest and upper-parts glossed blue-green, white nuchal cape scalloped with black feather-edgings, under-parts and tail white, the latter neatly barred with black and red tips to basal feathers. Long whitish legs noted.

The females appeared for only a short while; seen to be smaller and darker than ♀ Pheasant, with the horizontal carriage and richly-coloured plumage similar to Golden Pheasant.

E5 ———————————*November 30*———————— very cold, sunny

Lyng Gravel Pits, Norfolk   09.30

The female Red-crested Pochard located immediately on small lake with a few Pochard, Mallard and Tufted Duck.

A quite large, generally buffy-brown, duck with slightly paler flanks and tertials. Head with steep forehead and rounded crown, the dark brown crown and nape contrasting with the very pale, off-white, face. Longish bill grey with pinkish edges and tip.

Yare Valley, Norfolk   10.15

Party of 85 Bean Geese watched grazing over far side of marshes, several birds occasionally flying a short distance. Very large, dark geese showing well-marked upper-parts and contrastingly very dark head and neck. Head rather angular with long bill—patterned with black and orange. Long neck and wings noted in flight, the latter dark with minimal bluey cast on forewings.

No sign of the Cranes on the Broads; 25 Golden Plovers beside the road the only birds noted here.

Red-crested Pochard. Though escapes from captivity confuse the picture, this species appears to be a rare passage or winter visitor from Europe.

[180]

Bean Goose. Winter visitor in small numbers, with favoured traditional wintering sites in Solway, Northumberland and East Anglia.

Lowestoft Harbour, Suffolk   12.45

Four Purple Sandpipers feeding on wave-washed base of concrete pier wall. Very dark smoky-grey waders, with orangy legs and base to bill, most inconspicuous while on seaweed-covered rock. Flew into harbour, calling—short 'krutt' and 'treuk', etc., showing distinctive dark centre to rump and tail.

Several Kittiwakes seen perched on nests, this remarkable small colony being situated on the roof and window-ledges of a harbour-side warehouse.

Walberswick Marshes, Suffolk   14.15

Rather a lack of birds here except for 1 Sparrowhawk flying across the marsh and 1 ringtail Hen Harrier floating along far edge of marsh and over pines, flushing many Woodpigeons.

A brief stop at Harleston Gravel Pits produced only 30+ Tufted Ducks and 10+ Great Crested Grebes.

Purple Sandpiper. Mostly a winter visitor, favouring rocky coastlines but seen on passage in other coastal habitats.

[181]

Lowestoft Harbour, Suffolk
No sign of the Grey Phalarope which had been present over the previous few days, the only birds of note seen being several Sanderlings along the concrete sea-wall, and 1 adult Glaucous Gull perched on warehouse rooftop—this typically a large, mean-looking bird with heavy bill and white wing-tips reaching to just beyond tail.

Yare Valley, Norfolk
About 120 Bean Geese and 8+ White-fronted Geese feeding at far edge of marshes, seen at a little closer range than last week. Unlike the Beans, the White-fronts appeared rather unsettled, often flying around the marsh. Wigeon, Teal and Coots also grazing on the wet pasture.

Salthouse, Norfolk
A few Twite and Skylarks feeding on the gravel area behind the beach.
   The regular Glaucous Gull was hanging on the wind over the beach, and 40+ Brent Geese seen grazing at the Quags.

Pair of Eider. A resident, breeding commonly on the Scottish Islands and around the northern coasts, but occurring as a winter visitor, in small numbers, on coasts away from the breeding areas.

Wells, Norfolk
Several Twite and 1+ Lapland Bunting feeding in marshy area beside coast road, and a party of about 20 White-fronted Geese seen feeding in distant fields on Holkham Freshmarsh.

Titchwell, Norfolk
One male and 1 ringtail Hen Harrier floating around over reserve, together, and 15 Snow Buntings seen feeding among grassy tufts in sand-dunes on beach. A raft of about 150 Eiders offshore contained mostly female birds, but several immature ♂s with varied brown and off-white patterning and some good black and white ♂s.

[182]

Roydon Common, Norfolk

Two or three ♂ and 2 ringtail Hen Harriers came in to roost, sailing around over the common till dusk, the clean grey, black and white ♂s appearing quite a bit smaller than the brown-mottled females, both sexes showing a clear white rump-patch.

Three Merlins, including one adult ♂, seen dashing back and forth over the common during the evening, perching occasionally.

Also 1 Short-eared Owl seen, flying high over the back of the common, mobbed by a flock of Rooks.

December 24 cold, occasionally snowing

Swallow Moss, Staffs

Two Blackcocks flew over from copse, quite high, turning and apparently landing in distance. Very distinctive large glossy black grouse with lyre-shaped tail; quite long-winged, showing broad white wing-bar and flashing white under-wings and contrasting white under-tail coverts in flight.

Peak District, near Sheffield

Red Grouse (8+) seen on moorland close to the road—several flying and calling—distinctive gutteral 'gowk . . . . ok-ok-ok' or 'go-bak, go-bak' disappearing rapidly over the heather with bursts of quick wing-beats and long glides. On deck seen to be small, dumpy grouse with dark reddish-brown plumage barred all over with black. White wing-linings and feet also noted.

Black Grouse. Resident, breeding in suitable moorland-fringe habitats in most of Scotland and Wales, also parts of northern and south-western England.

[183]

Red Grouse. The characteristic bird of open moorlands in much of Wales, northern England and Scotland. Formerly regarded as the only truly endemic British bird, it is now classed as a race of the continental Willow Grouse.

Several Bramblings flew up from under roadside beeches, the white rumps distinctive even from a moving car.

Thetford, Norfolk   14.00

A pair of Mandarins seen on the river, feeding mostly near the bank under overhanging vegetation. The colourful orange, black and white drake rather overshadowing the grey-brown duck, its dull plumage relieved only by mottled under-parts and pale 'spectacles'.

Bill colour noted as pink on ♂, grey on ♀.

Mandarin, the most ornamental of all wildfowl, a firmly established introduced species with a feral population estimated at 300–400 pairs.

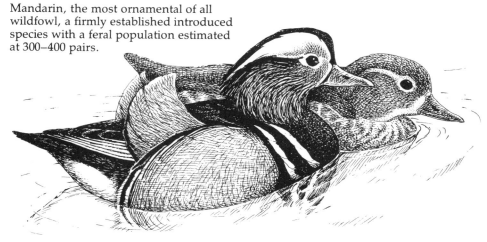

[184]

New Buckenham, Norfolk

Several Bramblings in the garden, and the resident Little Owl perched in usual trees alongside the nearby field, fluffed up into an almost spherical shape.

Two Woodcocks flushed from the common, one bird resting on a dry hummock under hawthorn bushes. Remarkably intricately patterned dead-leaf-camouflage plumage; a rich mixture of rufous, buff and black on upper-parts, lighter buff on under-parts, barred with dark brown. Broad dark bars on nape and large dark eye, set well back in head, also noted.

Woodcock. A widely distributed resident, breeding in most of Britain, with numbers swelled in winter by continental immigrants (when often seen in habitats other than the favoured mature woodlands).

Stackpole, Dyfed   08.00–09.30

The juvenile Cattle Egret was located feeding in field on hilltop, then watched at close range feeding around cows near farm. Also seen flying, and perched, rather precariously, on top of hedge.

A small, quite thick-set, egret; lumpy-looking with very slightly elongated crest and prominent 'jowl'. Plumage all-white at distance but showing a pale buff wash on the secondaries of left wing and slight buffish tinge to crown at close range. Relatively stout yellowish bill, yellow eye and dull pinkish legs (greyer towards dark feet) also noted.

One ♀ Sparrowhawk flew across road, flushing many finches from nearby fields, and 1 Grey Wagtail feeding along muddy track.

Nearby, at Bosherton Fish-ponds, 2 wintering Chiffchaffs watched feeding; flycatching from brambles in a sheltered, sunny corner with several Goldcrests.

Cattle Egret. The arrival of about 6 individuals this winter was quite remarkable, only 23 birds having been recorded previously in Britain. Though some individuals may escape from captivity, this species is widely distributed through southern Asia and Africa and is a strong erratic dispersive migrant. It has recently colonised much of South America, central America and eastern North America, also Australia, though the nearest colonies to Britain are around the Mediterranean.

[186]

INDEX OF SCIENTIFIC NAMES

This index contains references to all birds mentioned in the text, whether seen or not.

[188]

INDEX OF COMMON NAMES

This index contains references to all birds mentioned in the text, whether or not seen.

[191]